FROM CREW TO CAPTAIN

*Making the transition from working
for a big institution to
working for yourself*

By David Mellor

with original illustrations by James Mellor

www.davidmellormentoring.com

Filament
Publishing

Published by Filament Publishing Ltd
14, Croydon Road, Waddon,
Croydon, Surrey. CR0 4PA
Telephone +44 (0)20 8688 2598
Fax +44 (0)20 7183 7186
info@filamentpublishing.com

www.filamentpublishing.com

© David Mellor 2010

David Mellor asserts the moral right to be
identified as the author of this work.

Printed by Antony Rowe
Chippenham and Eastbourne

ISBN 978-1-905493-42-5

Introduction

The purpose of this book is to help people understand the transition from working for a big institution to working for themselves. I have made this journey, and helped many others do the same.

I want to put the odds in your favour, if you decide to follow suit, that your business venture brings you everything you wish, and that you prosper rather than merely survive. You will find inside a number of practical tips and hints, all garnered from the "University of Life".

It will draw on a broad range of interview material from people who have made or are making this journey, and for whom success has looked very different. It will also draw on a wealth of anecdotal evidence, from my own experience and that of others.

Our journey will take us through 3 important phases:

1. *Reflecting* - what does it take to make this transition - and is it for you?

2.   *Planning* - how do you go about preparing to launch your business?

3.   *Doing* - what attributes are going to be really important in the early days post-launch?

Foreword

David Mellor and I share a passion. Fairplace's very rationale is to help people decide what they want to do in their career and more importantly help them achieve their goals. Approximately 5,000 people work with us every year and about 10% set out on the voyage of establishing their own business. It is our obligation to our clients to ensure they understand it will not all be plain sailing; indeed to use the old adage: "Fail to prepare, prepare to fail".

David's ability is to cut through the rhetoric and hyperbole, and we have all read self help books that fail to self help, and give practical common-sense advice. But of course, we all know that commonsense isn't common, which makes this book a masterpiece. This book will ensure you understand the oceans you need to navigate; it will help you plot your route, really thinking through all the options, planning to make it happen. I have witnessed this on many occasions, as David works with his clients.

As a career coach of 15 years, nothing gives me as much pleasure as seeing my clients achieve their potential. Knowing that you have helped someone build their boat, seeing it launched, helping them navigate the rapids of day to day business and finally seeing them arrive at their destination port gives immense pleasure. It is that pleasure that David and I share.

Assuming you are reading this book as preparation to building your boat, I wish you luck. I know that the time spent reading and the money spent on the purchase will prove to be a sound investment, and of critical importance to ensure your boat is sea worthy.

Apologies for all the nautical references, but what can you expect from a book titled "From Crew to Captain".

Michael Moran
Chief Executive
Fairplace
14th January 2010.

About the Author

Prior to establishing his own consultancy practice in 2001, David Mellor had a 25-year career in banking with HSBC and Deutsche Bank. Spells in HSBC's UK branch network and in Deutsche's Venture Capital division gave him exposure to the small business market. Since 2001 he has capitalised on this and specialised in mentoring aspiring business owners, launching hundreds of people on this path, and on occasions persuading people not to do it! His approach is very simple – does the individual have the attitude and mindset to make the adjustment, does he/she have a proposition that makes sense, and what practical tips and hints do they need to help them launch with confidence and achieve success (whatever that means for them) rather than becoming just another casualty.

To Anne,

who has supported me on my journey since 1974, of which this book is just one tiny part.

Acknowledgements

This feels a bit like the Oscars, as there are so many people to thank.

Firstly, I would like to thank the team at Fairplace, particularly Michael Moran and Linda Jackson, who gave me the chance to create my own niche in this area.

Then there is Scott Moeller, a long-time business colleague at Deutsche Bank and Cass Business School, who has been badgering me for some time to do this.

I received invaluable help from Anne Caborn, who has a way with words way beyond my ability.

I would also like to thank the various "sponsors" who have contributed some highly valuable expert input to the book - Andrew Pullman, Lauren Conroy, Ed Simpson, Gordon Westcott and Duncan Hollands.

I am also indebted to a group of people who are all at different stages on this journey and who were prepared to be interviewed about their experience thus far. You will encounter their thoughts and comments as you work your way through the book. So my thanks go to Chris

Robinson, Christine Stedmann, Norman B Burnham, Lauren Conroy, Stuart Hillston, Mike Teasdale, Simon Cornelius, Vanessa Sammut, Kerwin Hack, Paul Fileman, Jon Sweet, Andrew Pullman, Simone Davis, Marc Oratis, Claire Brynteson and Stephen Willoughby.

I must also mention Marina Kapur, whose words of encouragement in the summer of 2009 gave me the courage to put pen to paper.

Then there is a whole host of people who have contributed anecdotal evidence; some have contributed on an anonymous basis, whilst others are named in the text.

A number of people took time out to proofread the text for me. I am therefore very grateful to Janice Rowsell, Peter Salisbury, Fiona Shafer, Ginette Sibley and Bob Silver. Fiona deserves a double "thank you" as she has been acting as my mentor for more years than she cares to remember!

My business partner, Stephen Furner, is to be thanked for being a source of reference and support as and when required.

Next to last is my long-suffering P.A. Vanessa, who has "lived" this process with me.

Finally, there is my family - Louisa, for her constant encouragement, James for his wonderful illustrations, and Anne for being there.

CONTENTS

Chapter 1 - Reflecting.................... 17
The Adjustment Process......................... 19
Options.. 33
Motivators.. 35
Personal Qualities.............................. 43
Chapter 2 - Planning....................... 57
Characteristics of a Successful Business...... 57
Business Skills Inventory....................... 67
Proposition....................................... 81
Market.. 85
Clients.. 85
Competition...................................... 87
Image... 93
Strategic Plan.................................... 97
Business Plan.................................... 101
Operations....................................... 107
Financial Plan................................... 115
Funding Strategy................................ 119
Why Small Businesses Fail..................... 123
Chapter 3 - Doing......................... 141
Awareness.. 141
Routes to Market................................ 143
Networking....................................... 145
Sales.. 155
Delivery.. 181
Monitoring....................................... 183
Epilogue...................................... 193
Top Tips...................................... 195
Other Useful Reading....................... 229

CHAPTER 1
Reflecting.....

If you have difficulty figuring out whether running your own business, however big or small, is for you, then you might find Edgar H Schein's "Career Anchors" helpful. "Career Anchors" is a self-assessment tool that helps you to manage your career choices. A quote from Schein will help to clarify this:

"There is overwhelming evidence that, in an increasingly complex and global world, individuals have to become more self-reliant. But you cannot be more self-reliant if you do not have a clear concept of what you are good at, what you value, and what motivates you. This self-image of competence, motives, and values is your "career anchor"".

For further information go to www.pfeiffer.com

CHAPTER 1
Reflecting.....
What is this book all about then...?

I thought it would be helpful to start with a little bit about the philosophy behind this book. Not only will that help you learn what is in store in the pages ahead, you will gain an insight into the person going on the journey with you.

You will quickly learn that I love lists (do not ask my wife about this!). So here is a list of the main reasons why the book has come into being:

- Since I left the corporate world in 2001, I have set up a consultancy in my own right, merged it with a bigger one and subsequently demerged it. I have now developed a "portfolio career" - more on that later - and have spent 8 years working with a whole range of people who have also left the corporate world and are trying to do their own thing in many different ways.
- I have specialised in mentoring owner-managed businesses from cradle to grave, i.e. anything from pre-revenue start ups, through people looking to raise debt and equity to grow, through to people looking to sell. So I can see beyond the start-up to the end game, whatever that looks like.

- My aim is to try to give you a whole host of ideas to go away and reflect on, and in addition to give you a set of practical tips and hints that, if you do go down this route, will put the odds in your favour that you will be successful rather than become a national statistic - 50% of small businesses, whatever type, do not last the first year and 80% don't last 5 years. I want you to be on the other side of those statistics if this is what you decide to do.
- There are a great number of books on this topic of starting your own business. Many of them focus on taking your idea to market. That is absolutely fine. But what if you don't have an idea or you have an idea but are not sure that running your own business is the right option for you? I want to make sure these aspects are given a fair hearing.
- A number of people whose opinion I respect have all independently told me I should do this, and eventually I could not deny the urge to write it any longer.

The Adjustment Process

The first thing I would like to share with you is the adjustment process, which I remember I went through back in 2001. It is quite a huge change, moving from working from a big institution to working for yourself, even if it is to be yourself plus others. One key part of the adjustment is linked to whether you engineered your own departure or it was engineered for you. Depending on what is happening to you at this moment in time some of these adjustments might strike a chord with you.

I am not going to dwell on these as they are now fading memories for me; they have been eclipsed by other more exciting events. The first one is the whole issue of working from home which is where most people start - they don't usually go out and rent an office, studio or workshop. I was used to working from home because of the nature of the job in my later years at Deutsche Bank; I was out of the country three weeks out of four and was conditioned to working from home before and after trips, particularly as I am not very good at getting off the redeye flight and performing effectively. I am pretty much a wimp and I can't cope with sleep deprivation; by lunchtime it's like I have been hit by a truck!

But I am much better going home, getting a couple of hours sleep, getting back in the right time zone, doing a bit of work and then on day two getting back into the swing of it rather than going into the office and being a superhero; it just does not work for me.

As Clint Eastwood would say before he shot people: "a man has got to know his limitations" and I knew what mine were!

So I was used to working from home and I was quite disciplined; I did not lapse into watching daytime TV unless it was golf (my Achilles heel), and then I could get the siren call of the TV. But there is a huge difference between doing it for the odd day here and there and it becoming a way of life.

As I said, not many people go out on day one and decide that they need an office, a studio a workshop, or whatever it may be; they start from home and figure out "what is what" so there is quite a significant transition from being in a buzzy office environment where you have noise, chatter, gossip and everything else going on, to being in a more tranquil setting at home. When I started my wife was (and still is) a school teacher and my kids were at secondary school, and they all went out together in the morning at 7:30; the earliest back was around

Our interviews showed that the Top 3 "Things we miss about Corporate Life" were:

1. *Community*

2. *Administrative and Financial Support*

3. *Benefits (plus security of regular payslip)*

5:30 in the evening. During that time the only interruption, (we live at the end of a quiet cul-de-sac) was the postman who used to pitch up at around 11 o'clock. I felt like an old man on neighbourhood watch, as, if he had not appeared by 11:30 I would peer through the curtains thinking "has he fallen off his bike?" and wondering whether he was alright. I needed to get out more!

It dawns on you, particularly if you are a gregarious animal and you like social interaction, that the only person who can do something about it is you; you can't sit at home fretting about it.

At the same time you notice that the phone does not ring as much, you don't get as many text messages or emails and the only post you get is either bills or junk!

So we need to find some ways for you to fill your time constructively and at the same time get you out of the house - research and networking (see later) will be big parts of this.

The second big change I remember was all of a sudden the infrastructure I had taken for granted was not there anymore. The two things that hurt me most were firstly research and secondly legal.

Our interviews showed that the Top 3 "Wish I had known" were:

1. How much time needed to be invested in marketing self and business

2. People - to be more discerning and less trusting (Particularly in terms of difference between what people promise and deliver) - also filtering out bad clients early

3. How hard it is to get paid

Because of the nature of my former job I was heavily dependent on research; Deutsche Bank had more research than you could ever imagine, and so if I wanted information on a country, a company, an industry, or a peer group, somebody somewhere would have it and I would just go and get it. All of sudden now I had two choices: either do it myself or pay someone else to do it, and that hurts!

The other, as I said, was legal. Again because of the job I used to review rafts of legal documentation; now all of a sudden I had to trust my paralegal skills or pay a lawyer to do it for me, and that hurts even more because lawyers are not cheap!

So you have to figure out how you plug all those gaps in your infrastructure that you have been so dependent on in your career so far. Nowhere is this more painful for somebody like me than in the world of IT.

There is a well known oxymoron - the IT help desk - which is up there with "military intelligence", "customer service", and "business ethics". All of a sudden if you have a situation where your printer won't listen to your computer, or it decides that today is the day it prints in Egyptian for fun, or it won't print in a straight

Sources of Encouragement

Story 1

I am a big fan of golf, and I remember hearing a story which concerns Gary Player. Gary Player was at his peak the same time as Arnold Palmer and Jack Nicklaus. They were the big three at the time and they won many of the main trophies between them. Gary won one particular tournament and in the post tournament interview with the media one of the journalists was brave enough to say to him *"do you think lady luck was on your side today?"*. The answer, reportedly, was: *"It is a really funny thing but the more I practice the luckier I get"*. I generally believe it is true - the more you work at something, the luckier you get and things break for you, so perseverance and tenacity are really important.

Story 2

The second story, which is something to cling onto in the dark days (and there probably will be some), concerns a person called Pablo Casals. Pablo Casals was arguably the greatest concert cellist the world had ever seen and I remember hearing him being interviewed in the 1970's. He was asked: *"you are in your 80's and you are acknowledged as the world's greatest concert cellist, but rumour has it you still practice for 8 hours a day; why do you put yourself through this?"*. His answer: *"I keep getting better"*.

Story 2 - continued

What an unbelievable attitude from somebody in their 80's who has not got to prove anything to anyone. I see people out there, day in day out, who have that kind of drive. People who have that level of determination, provided they have an idea that makes sense, are going to make things happen.

"If you can see it in your mind's eye, you can hold it in your hand"

Bob Proctor, Inspirational Speaker

line, or your computer just hangs there and does nothing, who are you going to phone?

If reliable IT is going to be important to you in your new role, then you may want to consider some form of maintenance agreement with a local service provider. It can get quite fraught if you need to print something off to take to a client or a prospect and you can't do it!

There are four major checkpoints which I want to draw to your attention, which come up as you go through this adjustment process. The first two are closely linked.

I have repeatedly seen with other people that if you have the right attitude and mindset to make the adjustment, and you also have a business idea that makes sense, then normally it's a case not of whether you are going to be successful but how long it is going to take. If people have ticked both those boxes and then applied themselves the right way, with 90% perspiration and 10% inspiration, they eventually make their own luck and things start happening for them; the big question is how long it will take, and can you fund yourself for that period of time.

The third checkpoint concerns mentors. I have seen a direct correlation between people who employ some kind of mentor and people who don't, in terms of their success as they go down this route. People who have a mentor from day one seem to find it easier generally to get going than people who don't.

It can be different things for different people depending on you, the business you are going into, the business skills you have and so on. It could be somebody you already know, where there is a significant level of mutual trust and respect, where you can open up to this person in confidence and where they can be that wise head or wise old owl whom you can use as an impartial sounding board. This person could be found in your social network or in your existing business network.

If not, it could be somebody who has done something similar to you i.e. gone into the same line of business. Therefore they know the world you are going into quite well, and can give you a great deal of sector knowledge; they may also have a useful rolodex of contacts to contribute.

It could be somebody who has successfully built a business of a different type or in a different sector; he or she can therefore anticipate what is going to happen next and consequently help you to prepare for that as you go through the "growing pains".

Mike Teasdale says:
"Find an honest mentor who you can talk to. Not a friend who will tell you what you want to hear, but someone that will - in a positive and constructive way - challenge and mentor you through the journey".

Finally it could be somebody who has a skill you don't have. I did a lot of work down in Brighton with early stage technology businesses, where quite often there was one founder. These people would be very technically competent, whatever their area of IT expertise was, but quite often at the expense of other skills.

One option for them was to identify a mentor who was strong on marketing and sales. Typically they had a product or service that was advanced and innovative, but they did not know how to commercialise it. So, having a mentor who could help them figure out how they could take their offering to market and maximise it made a lot of sense.

It will be a different answer for all of you. If there is nobody that springs to mind, just keep your antennae up as you come across people and figure out who might be able to do that job for you. As I said, I have seen a direct correlation between people who take this step and people who make the transition successfully.

I have to take "my own medicine" and have worked with a mentor for over 4 years now. Fiona has been a fantastic impartial sounding board and has been instrumental at helping me structure the portfolio career I now have and fully enjoy.

How many Options are there?

- _Buy an Existing Business_

- _Invest in an Existing Business_

- _Start a Business from Scratch_

- _Buy a Franchise_

- _Look for Contract Work_

- _Build a Consultancy Practice_

- _Go Freelance_

- _Create a Portfolio Career_

Figure 1.1

The fourth and final checkpoint is aspirations. It's important to remember that success for one person may mean something completely different to others going through the same transition.

If you try to define success by way of some kind of monetary target, it may well depend on how old you are, how far you are along your journey in life, the extent to which this is topping up a situation where you are already financially independent, the extent to which you are the main or secondary bread winner, and the impact of children i.e. are they yet to go to school and/or university? All of these factors will determine what success has to look like. Again keep this in mind, because it is going to be a key part of your plan.

Options

I really just wanted to try to capture up front the different approaches that can be caught under this "working for yourself" umbrella. This calls for another list! (See Figure 1.1).

What are the Motivators?

- *Personal Interest – doing something you like, something you are passionate about*
- *Direct reward for efforts*
- *Flexibility*
- *Work/life balance*
- *Quality of life*
- *Control own destiny*
- *Own Boss*
- *Independence*
- *Financial control*
- *Keeping busy*
- *No politics*
- *Stimulation*
- *Exploiting a gap in the market*
- *Using existing/new skills – the way you want to use them*
- *Fulfilment*
- *Fun*
- *Freedom*

Figure 1.2

All of these will be referenced at different points in the book, and there will be some follow-on Fact Sheets. (That is a promise!).

Motivators

Let's take stock for a minute.

Why would you want to do this? Are we all individually or collectively mad even thinking of setting up our own businesses?

Do you really want to give up the security of a regular, predictable salary? How do you feel about having to work to a survival budget until your business is fully functional?

It might help you to reflect on some of the reasons. (See Figure 1.2).

Let's consider a couple of these in more detail.

Firstly fulfilment; something I have seen over the last eight years is that people get a massive buzz and a sense of fulfilment out of having an idea, getting it onto paper, and then proving to themselves that they can actually go and do it. The money is almost secondary; I stress almost secondary! Proving to yourself that you don't need a big organisation and that you can do it on your own is hugely fulfilling.

Secondly, flexibility. This one is very important to me. My daughter, who is now 22, was 13 when I started my own business. She is a very talented athlete. At the age of 12 she was playing senior ladies hockey; put a stick in her hand and she is frightening!

She went on to captain club, school and county; she also played at university, both at Durham and at the University of California. A number of her matches were during the week, when I could be in Singapore, or New York, but certainly not in downtown Reigate. All of a sudden now, if I could organise my diary, I could take the afternoon off. If that meant I had to work in the evening or part of the weekend, that was my call - I was the boss!

There is no better feeling as a parent than watching one of your kids doing something that they really enjoy and excel at; what made me sorry was that my son was about to go off to university; he was a very talented rugby player and I had missed many opportunities to see him play during the week. It is something you can't put a price on financially, so this benefit became really important to me.

Thirdly, exploiting a gap. Now most people going down this route will probably either be doing something differently or better than

Our interviews showed that these were the most common motivators:

1. *Fulfilment*

2. *Flexibility*

3. *Exploiting a Gap*

current providers. Occasionally you will find someone who will be exploiting a gap. I had the pleasure of meeting one such lady early in my mentoring career, called Claire Brynteson. Her business idea, which she developed whilst working in the world of investment banking, was shaped by her own needs and the glaringly obvious needs of everyone around her.

Claire never felt in control of her own life and it was the simple things that she found hard to juggle alongside her working days and the pressure of having too much to do with too little time was getting on top of her. Her dry cleaning, car services, household repairs, bill paying and paperwork, organising holidays, birthday presents, cleaning carpets etc. She realised that she needed a helping hand in life, one pro-active, competent person who could float in and take over when she needed her to and disappear again without cost when she didn't.

Claire had concierge services on offer at work as an employee benefit, although that didn't help. She didn't need to secure a last minute table at a top London restaurant and didn't need theatre tickets that often. She needed someone with keys to her house, based nearby and armed with a kitty who could go shopping, meet and oversee the plumber at home, book some flights, feed the cat whilst she was away and at the same time, get rid of that ever increasing paper mountain (as she created the filing system in the first place), take the husband's shoes for repair and organise a replacement oven.........getting the picture? She had a constant list the length of her arm that felt stressful to even think about.

A smart, dedicated yet flexible and cost effective personal assistant, to enable all busy people to stay on top of things and actually relax and enjoy their precious time outside work.

There were hundreds of employees at the company Claire worked at, who she knew would welcome a service of this kind and that was only one company in only one town. There was obviously an enormous market and Claire had an excellent idea to put in front of it. She called her venture buy-time.co.uk and she did not charge her customers any membership fees nor did she ask them to commit to any particular usage. She gave them a dedicated assistant in life that they paid for by the hour. She offered discounts to customers purchasing blocks of hours in advance, to have on account and gave them a full year to use the hours.

Claire says: "it really was just what I needed for myself and consequently I have used the services of my own company ever since".

Her company buy-time.co.uk has developed into providing business support solutions to entrepreneurs, sole traders and small to medium sized businesses. Professionals and companies now may outsource their administration to exactly fit their requirements and save themselves all the ongoing costs of hiring an individual. In addition, these customers have the freedom of a virtual PA, who can also work from the customer home or office and also run errands, attend meetings and travel on business trips. She manages rental properties and private households too, giving a combined, comprehensive helping hand and really freeing the customers to focus on their businesses.

So, it can be seen that when a gap is spotted, an effective idea can become a pulsating, growing business and with the right people, at the right time, the business can continue to go from strength to strength.

Personal Qualities

- *Personable*
- *Good Listener*
- *Organised*
- *Tenacious*
- *Energetic*
- *Streetwise*
- *Discerning*
- *Sense of Humour*
- *Self-Aware*
- *Resilient*
- *Conscientious*
- *Empathetic*
- *Resourceful*
- *Analytical*
- *Finisher*
- *Positive*

Figure 1.3

Personal Qualities

There is a big list (see figure 1.3) but there are five others that I consider to be particularly important.

The first of these is **Integrity**. Irrespective of what you call your business, you and it are joined at the hip from day one. And as in all walks of life, it takes a long time to build a positive reputation, but you can lose it in a heartbeat.

My dear old dad use to say "treat others like you expect to be treated" and that really rings true in running your own business.

Corporations talk about values and principles, and that should hold good for you; it is important that you live out your personal code of conduct in your business, and build a reputation based around trust and reliability. You do not want to have a reputation for:

- Promising something then failing to follow-up or deliver.
- Turning up late for meetings, or not turning up at all.
- Being a difficult (as opposed to tough) negotiator.
- Being a bad payer.

So integrity is vital in my work and it will be in yours.

Next comes *passion*. If you can't be passionate about what it is you are going to be doing, then don't expect anyone else to be. One of the things that you have to do is make the passion for what you do and what you represent contagious. That should be one of your overriding objectives. You should also know where you draw the line so that you do not step over it and become overbearing!

I used to encounter a certain business owner on the networking circuit who regularly abused the privilege of having a relatively "captive" audience. As a result people would go out of their way not to talk to her as she just did not know when to stop. She did not know when the passion turned into her being an irritant. You need to know where the boundary is.

That leaves three more qualities, which hang together very well. A little story for you on the following pages (Figure 1.4) illustrates the importance of *Vision*, rock-solid *Belief* and *Determination*. The story is about Leadership; even if the business is just yourself, you are leading it!

Sources of Encouragement

Story 3

You all know that Nelson Mandela spent a significant part of his life in prison, and most of that was in solitary confinement; I think it was about 27 years. Apparently there is a house in Soweto, where Nelson Mandela lived when he was little. This house has now been turned into a tribute to him. It apparently contains a range of Nelson Mandela memorabilia, from the baby, toddler, junior school, secondary school, university, prison and presidential periods of his life. One of the first groups to go around this house was a group of locals, and included in the group was a forensic scientist. He reached the prison part of the display and found a pair of shoes; he said to the host "are these Nelson Mandela's?" and the host said "yes". He said he had never seen shoes with this sort of wear and tear, and asked to borrow them so that he could run some tests. The tests were duly done, and his findings were that the only thing that could generate this sort of wear and tear was running on the spot. The forensic scientist asked whether Nelson Mandela had done a lot of running on the spot in prison. The host had no idea but investigated and reported back that he had indeed. "Where is this story heading?", you may ask.

Figure 1.4

The story I heard was attributed to Archbishop Desmond Tutu and concerns Nelson Mandela, a leader the Archbishop obviously knows well.

The challenge the Archbishop reportedly threw out to his audience, was that these qualities, evidencing inspirational leadership, could be applied to any leader, even one running a small business. So:

- Do you have a vision for your business i.e. can you picture what success is going to look like for you?
- Do you have the belief you can make it happen?
- Are you determined to give it your best shot?

That was the message that everyone took away with them, the challenge is the same for me, and for all of you.

Sources of Encouragement

Story 3 – continued

To cut to the end of the story, basically what happened was that when Nelson Mandela was in prison he had a vision. This was not a visit from a celestial angel, but rather that he could picture in his mind a world where there was a unified South Africa and he was the first black leader. Furthermore he could picture this as a reality in his lifetime. Having pictured it he had a rock solid self belief that if he had the chance, he could do the job. He was a realist and knew he could be quite advanced in years before he got the opportunity and that he needed to be in the best physical and mental shape to take on the challenge, so he had the drive and determination to make sure that if he did get the chance he could give it his best shot. In terms of keeping his brain sharp there was not too much of an issue as he had access to writing materials, so he could write and he had access to reading materials, so he could read. However, apart from one brief spell in a quarry breaking rocks, most of his time was spent in his cell and he was not allowed to use the exercise yard. So what he did was run on the spot in his cell for 4 hours a day to keep fit.

Figure 1.4 (continued).

To reinforce this I want tell you another story about someone I have worked with and who has become not just a business associate but a good friend. Her name is Christine and her story is on the following page. (Figure 1.5).

If you need motivation or inspiration, Christine is a great example for you; particularly if the thing that is worrying you is "Can I do it?"

Sources of Encouragement

Story 4

In 2008 I met Christine Stedmann at Fairplace. Christine had worked for one of the major UK banks. Her parting from the bank had not been a particularly pleasant experience, so when I meet her she was still recovering from the whole redundancy process, and her morale and self esteem were pretty low. I describe her natural style as a bit like "Tigger on caffeine" - she is bright and bubbly, so this was not the real Christine I have come to know. However, she had a vision; she wanted to set up a business, she had a vision of what she wanted her business to look like; she called it Zentime. (Competition to Claire Brynteson, but competition is healthy).

I worked with her over the summer, helping her to write her business plan, and she launched in September 2008. She had as much drive and determination as anyone I have ever met. Where she was struggling was the third component; where she needed rock-solid belief, she had self doubt, and thought to herself; "can I actually do this"?

She launched 1st September and the first month was a disaster. She had no hits on her website. No calls; nothing happened.

Figure 1.5

Sources of Encouragement

Story 4 - continued

In October 2008 it all changed and there was one development that tripped the whole process. She was featured in the Guardian as someone going through the "reinvention" process.

The article told her story, and how she got through the difficult period. From thereon she has not looked back, and is well and truly back to being "Tigger on caffeine". She now has the belief. The vision and the determination she already had, but the belief was the missing thing. It took the article to help her get the belief back, it was there but somewhat buried. She has now gone from strength to strength, and is a living example of why these three leadership attributes are so important.

SELF-DIAGNOSTIC ONE
Are you finished with your reflection phase?

NO	ISSUE	SCORE out of 10
1	Are you comfortable with not having a regular predictable salary?	
2	Have you worked out your survival budget?	
3	Are you confident you can exceed your survival budget?	
4	Are your family supportive of your plans?	
5	Have you taken sufficient advice on your idea?	
6	Do you have a vision of what you want your business to look like?	
7	Do you have the self-belief that you can make that vision a reality?	
8	Do you have the drive and determination to make it happen?	
9	Are you passionate about your idea?	
10	Has anyone stress-tested your business idea for viability?	
TOTAL		

Score < 30 *You may want to rethink whether this is for you*

Score < 60 *You may want to revisit some of these issues before you make a go/no-go decision*

Score > 60 *You probably have enough momentum to proceed to the planning phase.*

<u>SELF-DIAGNOSTIC ONE</u>

You are now ready to take the first test (facing page) - are you done reflecting?

CHAPTER 2
Planning...

CHAPTER 2
Planning ...
Characteristics of a Successful Business

It is important to make the point that some of these make sense even if you plan to work completely on your own.

The first characteristic is that, on the day they start the business, the owners know how they are going to end it, i.e. they have an exit strategy. The other decision they need to make at the same time is whether they are going to be running a value business or a lifestyle business.

If you set a business up in a way that you take out every penny it makes and you use that to pay for what you and your family need today and maybe put some on one side for what you and your family need tomorrow, then the likelihood is that on the day you decide to stop, it stops as it is of no value to anybody else. There is nothing there of value anyone can buy. It has funded your lifestyle.

If on the other hand you take out what you and your family need today, and maybe something that you can put towards what you and your family need tomorrow, but the rest you plough back into product development, research, acquiring other small businesses, geographic

Our interviews showed that:

Over 70% had a clear vision, although in some cases the picture changed based on experience (usually for the better).

expansion, opening new offices, creating intellectual property or toolkits and methodologies, then the likelihood is that you are actually creating a value business that somebody else in the future may want to buy off you. It does not matter which you are just as long as you know, and plan your finances accordingly!

One of the reasons why my colleagues and I have been so busy as a consultancy is that approximately 80% of people who set up their own business do not have an exit strategy. In addition, some of them believe they are a value business when in fact they are a lifestyle business.

I recall one business owner whom we met when he was 52; his game plan was to retire at 57, sell the business, buy a property in the Mediterranean, fly south with the birds for the Winter, then come back in the Spring. We were chatting away and he was asked what the required capital sum was for this retirement lifestyle, and he had no idea. What about pension? Well the business was his pension. Did he know what the business was worth? Again no idea. Would it not be a shame, he was asked , if in five years time he found that the business could not be sold for the capital sum needed, or even worse couldn't be sold at all, which would mean that he would have to keep working. So we offered

Paul Fileman says:
"Make sure you can fund 12 months without earning. Spend wisely on your own marketing plan early in the process - whilst you still have reserves. Identify a niche and operate within that niche. Be prepared to give your time away in the early days to gain references.".

to help him create a value business, and fortunately we had the timescale to do it.

There is a time bomb ticking in situations like this, where people sometimes live in a world of illusion, where they consider the business to be a retirement nest egg, when in fact it is worth little or nothing. Certainly it is often not worth what they think it is and in many cases the value walks out with them! Successful businesses have figured this out up front and plan accordingly. There is nothing wrong with a lifestyle business provided you take out the money wisely. There is not a right or wrong situation; you just have to understand the implications of the way you choose to run it.

The second characteristic is that the owners reach a stage where they are managing "on" the business rather than "in" it; they have an opportunity to see what is going on around them and can react accordingly.

The third characteristic is that they only spend money on what is in the budget. They have a vice-like grip on the cash both in and out.

The fourth characteristic is that they build the business around systems, not people. By that I don't mean that people are not important, but people work much better if they know the

SALES PROCESS

Figure 2.1

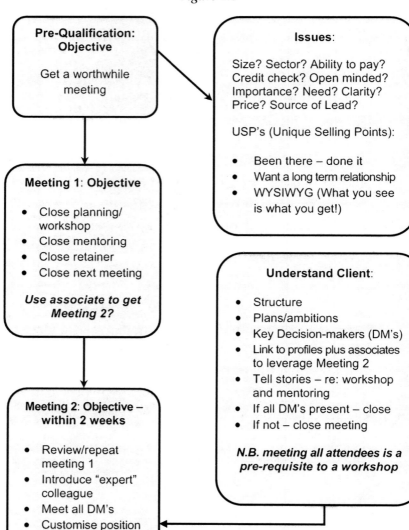

Pre-Qualification: Objective

Get a worthwhile meeting

Issues:

Size? Sector? Ability to pay? Credit check? Open minded? Importance? Need? Clarity? Price? Source of Lead?

USP's (Unique Selling Points):

- Been there – done it
- Want a long term relationship
- WYSIWYG (What you see is what you get!)

Meeting 1: Objective

- Close planning/ workshop
- Close mentoring
- Close retainer
- Close next meeting

Use associate to get Meeting 2?

Understand Client:

- Structure
- Plans/ambitions
- Key Decision-makers (DM's)
- Link to profiles plus associates to leverage Meeting 2
- Tell stories – re: workshop and mentoring
- If all DM's present – close
- If not – close meeting

N.B. meeting all attendees is a pre-requisite to a workshop

Meeting 2: Objective – within 2 weeks

- Review/repeat meeting 1
- Introduce "expert" colleague
- Meet all DM's
- Customise position
- Close/sign LOE (Letter of Engagement)

Don't:

Explain process
Give sample results
Give free advice

process they are supposed to be following. That applies in two areas:

- How you win clients in the first place, i.e. you need a sales process
- How you keep clients happy so that they will buy from you again and/or recommend others to use your product or service i.e. you need a delivery process

If you look at the facing and following pages (Figure 2.1 and Figure 2.2) you will see the *sales process* and *delivery process* that I use in my consultancy. We have learned the hard way that if we skip any of the stages in the sales process it will come back and bite us in the backside - we end up with either a timewaster or a potential bad debt! I am not saying you should slavishly follow what we have, it's just to give you an idea of the kind of process you might find useful if you decide to go down this route. Whether you are going to be selling a product or a service, think about what would be the equivalent process for you and then, even it is only going to be you, document the procedure and follow it. It's not complicated.

We follow it, and we are well aware that if we depart from it we increase the risk of storing up a problem for ourselves.

DELIVERY PROCESS

Figure 2.2

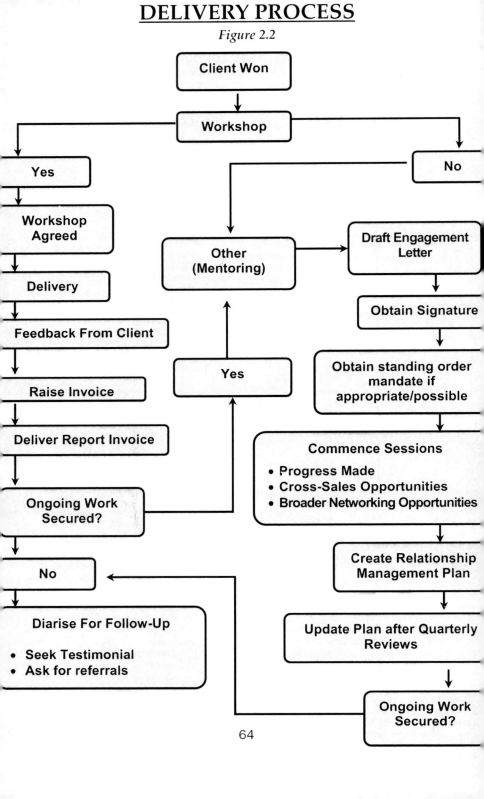

If anybody else then joins you, be it as a new member of staff, a strategic partner, or an associate, you can show them and say quite simply "This is the way we do things"; you don't need a 60-page operations manual, you just need something like this. I would encourage you to do this, even if it's just you that is following it and nobody else.

We will talk more about the sales process in the next chapter; suffice to say at this stage that it helps you to weed out the time wasters and bad debts; with the delivery one, you increase the chance you have a satisfied client who comes back and/or refers other people to you.

And, by the way, it is much easier to build a business from quality referrals and recommendations than it is having to go out cold all the time to try and find new customers.

Business Skills Inventory

- *Know your market (technical skill)*
- *Basic IT Skills*
- *Basic understanding of accounts*
- *Basic bookkeeping*
- *Invoicing*
- *Cash management – both creditors and debtors*
- *Forecasting*
- *Budgeting*
- *Tax/VAT/National insurance etc*
- *Sales*
- *Marketing*
- *Networking*
- *Planning*
- *Communication (verbal and written)*
- *Time Management*
- *Legal*
- *HR*
- *Management Skills*
- *Project Management*
- *Negotiation Skills*
- *Logistics*
- *Procurement*
- *Relationship Management*

Figure 2.3

Business Skills Inventory

This is a good time to take stock of our business skills inventory; bearing in mind we have in all likelihood left a business world where we had developed specialised functional skills. Now, this piece is very important. One of my famous lists is on the facing page. (See Figure 2.3) What I suggest you do is go through the list as an inventory and don't cheat - be honest - and ask yourself; "is that something I can do?". If not, is it something it would be sensible to invest in and get trained, or is it something where it would be sensible to outsource to someone else? If you actually duck any of them, or persuade yourself that you can do it when in fact you can't, it may well prove to be the "Achilles Heel" of your business and come back and haunt you at a later stage.

This list is highly relevant, whether the business is going to be just you or more than you. I will reinforce the point by referencing "The Beermat Entrepreneur", written by Mike Southon & Chris West. This is a great little book which starts with five guys setting up a company and dividing the roles up between them.

The company they set up sees them each with 20% of the equity, so there is no argument over who earns what. They divvy up the jobs

between them based on what they are good at and what they enjoy doing. They are all capable of doing more than one thing but there are five of them, so how is it shared out?

They start with a great networker, who can go out and be very ambassadorial, press the flesh, make people aware of the business, what makes it different, and generate leads. They are not necessarily the best salesperson but they are brilliant at getting out there and making the world at large aware that the business exists. This person is supported by what Mike and Chris call "Cornerstones".

The first is the creative; he comes up with the first product or service based on market needs, and whilst that is being marketed he develops the next product or service.

The second is the sales person who will go out, selling what the creative has come up with and capitalising on the awareness that the networker has created.

Then you have the operations person who deals with everything post sale. So getting the right product to the right person, on the right day, in the right location and dealing with all the administration.

Our interviews showed that the Top 3 "Good News Items" were:

1. *Being own boss/being in control*

2. *Sense of fulfilment*

3. *Freedom from politics*

The final one is the finance person who keeps a vice like grip on the cash in and out. So, that is the way they share out the roles and responsibilities.

A set-up like this is really important if you are intent on building a business that is scalable and capable of sustainable profitable growth.

If, on the other hand, you have no aspirations for the business to be anything other than you, it's still valid because you are in the position that you have to do all of these jobs. Part of the time you could be out increasing the awareness, part of the time you are thinking about what your service or product should be, part of the time you are selling it, part of the time you are delivering it, and then part of the time you are watching the money coming in and out. So you have to be able to fulfil all five roles, or seek help from somebody else, otherwise you will find it hard to get the business off the ground.

So it's equally valid in all circumstances - it's just you have to wear all the hats though. You can't just do the bit that you like, or the bit you think you are good at; you have to ensure you deal with the other components yourself or courtesy of someone else. Hugely important!

Stephen Willoughby
says:
"You can never do too much research before commencement".

Now let's go back to what I call the "technical skill". Small businesses fail because they run out of cash. That is about as helpful as saying the patient died because he stopped breathing. It's 100% accurate but it tells you nothing at all.

There are many different ways that a small business will run out of cash, and I will come back to this later but before we do that, the biggest reason by far - the banks and insolvency practitioners have all done studies on this - that small businesses or business start ups fail, is that the owner or owners who started it did not know what they were getting into. They did not understand their market; they went into it "eyes wide shut". You would be amazed how many people do that and just assume that they know better, and quite often they don't. That is the main reason small businesses fail. Other reasons spin off from this, but the main reason is often that they quite simply did not know what they were getting into.

I want to give you a few case-studies of people I have encountered over the years, it might help you to decide where you are on the risk spectrum, and then you can react accordingly. I call this *low, medium and high risk.*

Low Risk Case

The first one was a sprightly young man of 64 years; he had left school at 16, and had spent his entire life in the shipping industry, becoming a Health and Safety expert. Shipping is quite a small market, and he was well known. Furthermore, what he did not know about health and safety in shipping was not worth knowing. At 64 he had parted company with his employers, but decided he still had something to give. He was going to set up his own consultancy, providing health and safety advice in the shipping business. He had 48 years experience, everybody knew him; he knew everyone else; he knew how the market worked, so he could go in "eyes wide open". This is a low risk start-up. He was taking all the skills and experience he had accumulated and was applying them in a market he knew and which knew him.

Medium Risk Case

Medium risk is where you can apply everything you have learned so far but you are going to try and apply it in a market that you don't know and which does not know you. I met two brothers who had both worked in IT in one investment bank for their entire careers - they were in their early to mid 40's.

Medium Risk Case - continued

They were looking to set up their own company and they were going to offer virtual IT services support to small and medium sized companies that needed an IT director but could not justify a full time role either financially or time wise. I see this as medium risk because they knew their stuff but they were going into a market that they did not know and that did not know them. I had no doubt they could deliver, because they had the technical expertise, but my concern was whether they actually had the mix of personal skills to sell themselves. We will come back later to the attributes of a sales person, and networking and their relative importance to building a business.

High Risk Case

High risk is where everything you have learnt thus far is not directly relevant to your business idea, and in addition you are going in to a market you don't know and which does not know you. This is really where you need to make sure that you have done your research before you start, so that you go in "eyes wide open". I have two examples for you.

High Risk Case - continued

The first one was a lady who from memory was a junior in the fixed income operations area of an investment bank. She said that she had a one-off opportunity to turn her hobby into a business.

This normally scares me, (alarm bells - potentially high risk) but I asked her to elaborate. Her passion was her garden and she had decided to open a florist shop. What this lady did is quite remarkable, and I can't take any credit as she had already done it by the time she had come to my attention. Imagine she lived south of London, in a "commuter town", so Guildford, Leatherhead, Dorking, that kind of area. She identified that in the high street there was no florist; she further identified there was a vacant retail outlet in a good spot in the high street. She then did some Googling and found a commuter town due north of London and on the M25 where there was a florist in the high street. She telephoned; a man answered and she outlined her plan, said she was no threat to his business as she was so far away, and she asked whether if she came to see him, he would share his experiences with her. The man agreed and they met.

High Risk Case – continued

He told her everything - the mistakes he made; the things he would do differently second time around; how to fit the shop out; where to source materials for the fit-out, and likely cost; how to deal with suppliers and what tricks they played; what margins were available, promotional ideas that worked; dealing with seasonal issues, Christmas, Easter, Mother's Day, Valentine's Day; how to deal with deliveries. He explained about footfall count and the average amount people spent; this is hugely important if you think about it, as if you go into a florist you have already decided you are going to buy some flowers - it's not like going into a clothes shop and browsing. So the footfall count is quite a good predictor of how many people you would expect to come in and the average amount that they would spend.

Armed with this data her next step was to head south and sit in a cafe on the high street, from which she could see her potential shop; she sat there all day Monday, all day Wednesday, all day Friday and all day Saturday. Monday was quiet, Wednesday was market day, Friday was really busy and Saturday was a typically manic high street day. Four different profiles in terms of footfall.

High Risk Case – continued

Monday to Friday she also stayed on into the evening, so she could pick up the commuter traffic coming home and see how many of them passed the shop. Now she had the data she could map it against the conversion ratios that the North London florist had told her. She also had the pricing model, and a costing model, so she could now create a set of assumptions from which she could create her financial forecasts and subsequently create a business plan.

She then went to the bank and said she was interested in taking the lease on the property, so that she could open a florist. She showed them her calculations, indicating that her savings and redundancy money would cover 50% of the start up costs and 50% of the year one operating costs without selling anything and asked the bank to match fund her, which they did. I can guarantee you that banks are not used to seeing a pre-revenue start-up submit a plan of that calibre with such robust assumptions that could be defended; moreover she had gone out of her way to eliminate, or at least reduce the technical risk.

Contrast her approach with that of an investment banker I met.

He was, articulate, well dressed and supremely confident. He was going to sell his property and move to Cornwall and run a guest house. When questioned about whether he knew much about the guest house business he said that he had stayed in one once..... Enough said.

Before we move on, a final little story, which I hope you will find encouraging. It concerns an Italian lady who had worked for one of the Italian banks in London, and had been made redundant. She was going to import ladies luxury goods from Milan and was trying to get a concession in one of the West End stores; she identified her skills gap and did two very interesting things. Firstly she went to Petticoat Lane market and went up to three East End "geezers"; she asked them if she fetched their coffee and teas and sandwiches all day could she watch how they went about selling shirts! To have the courage to face your fears and do something about them is a mark of a business leader; it contributes to you making your own luck, and you deserve to be successful. The second thing she did was to be taken on by one of the high street retail chains. She worked on a short fixed term contract at a very modest wage but had exposure to every aspect of running a retail operation – ordering,

PROPOSITION

Avoid jargon. You will be amazed at the number of people who blow their own feet off using jargon. I was grooming someone to go in front of the real life Dragons' Den; my objective was simple - help him go forward into a business angel environment and come out with a cheque rather than in a body bag or on a stretcher. He had a First from Oxford and a Masters from Sussex and told me he was an expert in neural networks. I just looked at him. We got off to a horrible start and I threw him out (in a nice way) and told him to come back when he could tell me what he did in words I would understand.

Use doing words, not descriptors. It makes your description more dynamic! I met a lady at a networking event, who introduced herself as a trained hypnotherapist and NLP practitioner. The eyes of the entire room of 40 people glazed over. Nobody knew what a NLP practitioner was. Not only had she used jargon, she had put herself in a "box". The people who ran the event took her to one side and said, "Look, if you are going to make the most of this, you have to make it easy for people to know what you do, so if you don't want people to look blank, you have to change what you say". The next week she came back and to her credit had changed her pitch, she began with "if you are scared of flying, I can help you with that; if you are trying to lose weight, or stop smoking I can help you with that".

Figure 2.4

inventory control, store layout, handling complaints and so on.

People like this deserve to succeed!

Proposition

It is really important that you can articulate with absolute clarity what your business proposition is. This is vital because, unless you are really fortunate, there will not be many occasions when you meet somebody for the first time who is ready at that moment to buy what you do, and you will meet two types of people - those who at some stage might buy your product or service, and those who can refer to you people who might buy your product or service; some people could fall into both categories. It is therefore essential that you can communicate what you do, both verbally and in print, so that it is easy for the listener or reader to grasp what you do. I have put some hints on the facing page. (See figure 2.4).

PROPOSITION – *continued*

She then went on to explain that she had certain qualifications which gave her the ability to offer this. She had come up with a much more successful way of getting her proposition over to an audience. Something which I did not realise until recently was that, when you talk to somebody, they open in their brain a folder with your name, company name and what you do in it. If they can come up with a helpful image they will put that in as well. So our NLP practitioner did exactly that – everybody could picture a plane, a cigarette, a piece of cake, a spider or any other phobia and they could create a record that she was someone who could deal with that. By the way, my accountant changed his pitch from "I am an accountant" to "I help businesses owners make more money and pay less tax". He told people what he did as opposed to what he was.

Understand why people might buy from you. If your market is "business to consumer" there is a whole variety of reasons why people might buy from you, and you have to build that into your description of yourself. It could be convenience, peace of mind, security, safety, fashion or a range of other features. You have to make sure your message taps into the right one so that you get the recall.

PROPOSITION – *continued*

If on the other hand your market is "business to business" there is only one reason why they are going to buy from you and that is money. If you cannot get into your message that you are going to make money for people, save them money, or both, the likelihood is that the recall level will be lower as sooner or later they will have to link it to a budget that somebody has to approve. When I first started in consulting we used to say we helped business owners set and achieve their strategic objectives. People just used to look at us blankly - what does that mean? I changed it and now say we help people make money and free up their time. So the antennae go up and they ask, "How do you do that", and then you are in a conversation. All they needed to know was that we could do something that makes or saves them money, because that is the return on investment for them taking our service.

Create one page of A4 (in a sensible typefont) that captures the essence of what you do. This can also go on to form a key component of your website (more on that later), and the content of your elevator pitch (more on that also).

Test your proposition on a twelve year old. A twelve year old should have reached a level of literacy where, if you avoid jargon, he or she should be able to understand what you say and faithfully play it back to you to demonstrate the fact. If you put jargon in, they won't be able to do so.

Market

The next task is really making sure that your proposition is a solution to a problem, rather than the other way round, otherwise it's going to be hard work. In other words, are there sufficient people out there who are likely to buy your product or service, so that you have a viable business? Very closely linked to this is understanding the market, and researching trends and dynamics in the market - is it declining, steady or growing? Is it going to be here for all time or is it transitory?

Clients

Next comes the carbon-based life form known as the client. Who are your potential clients going to be - one homogeneous group or many different groups with different characteristics? Can you profile them? Can you establish who they are, where they are, what do they buy, how do they buy, why do they buy and so on. One of the key things to do as part of the research is to ask yourself the question: "If I decided not to do this and I went off to do something else, what would these people do? What would their alternative be? Would they be doing nothing, or would they be using an inferior product or service?" That would give you the benchmark that you would need to match and hopefully beat. This is a good way of looking at it.

Competition

My definition of competition is anyone or anything that prevents you from winning business; I think there are six categories.

1. People you go head to head with, where it is a straight fight on service or product quality and price.
2. People out there who could be confused with you. Because if you can be confused with somebody else, either by the way they describe themselves or by what they are called, then that confusion could be sufficient in the potential buyer's mind to increase the risk they don't buy from you. An example for my world: if I am at a networking event and do a particularly bad job of articulating what I do, I can guarantee you that somebody will assume that I am a coach. I am not a coach, I have no coaching qualifications, and I would never portray myself as a coach, but the very fact that people might mistake me for a coach can be a problem, as I have to explain why I am not a coach and what I actually am and do. I have to get back to zero before I can start selling. That is what I mean by being clear who you are and what you do.

3. "Closet competition" which is people who do what you do, and operate in your geographic patch, but win all of their business from word of mouth referrals; they do not have a website, and operate "off the radar" but they could be taking business you could otherwise win. Competition is therefore not just what you can see around you.

4. Overlap. This is people who do partly what you do, but the overlap is sufficient for them to be competition. Example from my world is the accountancy profession. We have had over the years many conversations with accountants and tried to build strategic relationships with them. We have said, "Look, you have clients with a whole range of needs, one of which is finance; if we teamed up, you could do the finance aspects and we could deliver some of the other aspects." I spent some time working with a consultancy that was very strong horizontally - we had consultants who were strong on marketing, sales, human resources, operations, IT, finance, and so on - anything you would expect to see on the board of a company we had people who could do that. Most consultancies go deep the other way, i.e. they will be experts at marketing, sales, finance, human resources, logistics, IT, etc. We used to

promote the "virtual board concept", i.e. if an entire board got wiped out in a plane crash we could put a complete set of replacements in and run the business. A very powerful message. The accountancy profession tended to look at us and conclude that we were competition, as we had finance people. We would counter that, we were happy to do everything else, apart from the finance, but most accountants remained reluctant to work with us and as a result a potentially lucrative route to market was largely closed to us.

5. Internal. This is particularly important if you are trying to get into the consultancy or contract space in IT or HR, as these are two disciplines where companies can move between choosing to outsource or bringing the work in house. Depending on where a company is on its cycle, you can either get business or lose business.

6. Inertia. The potential client chooses to do nothing. I can only think of a couple of recent examples where I have pitched for business and not won it. I can however think of many examples where people have decided to do nothing and just take their chances. Inertia is a huge, huge challenge. If the prospective client decides to do nothing, then in my book it's competition because it stops you getting

Our interviews showed that the Top 3 "Things you would do differently" were:

1. *Create more headroom in plan, be more realistic re time and cash necessary to build a viable business*

2. *More research*

3. *Surround self with good people in whatever capacity - partner, service provider, associate...*

business. How do you deal with client inertia? You will all face it, whether you are selling a product or a service. You need to have a disciplined diary system so that you can follow-up effectively on anything when the answer from the prospect is "yes, but not now".

I will conclude this section with a little exercise that you might find helpful to refine your proposition. See the following page. (Figure 2.5).

Research Exercise

We started off by talking about what your product or service is. There will probably be some assumptions at this stage. Once you have done that you are in a position to go and talk to a few people, wearing your research hat, who are potentially going to be clients. You could take some soundings at this stage by asking potential clients what they think of your offering, how does it fit with other offerings, are there any gaps it does not address? Because you are in research mode people are more likely to talk to you and give you an honest view.

Armed with that you can then start thinking about who you are competing with; people now put so much information on their websites in terms of who their clients are, what they offer, what makes them different, case studies, testimonials and so on; you can get a pretty good handle on what is being offered.

If you test your assumptions with potential clients, and then benchmark your assumptions against your competition you may find that you can tweak what you offer to your advantage.

You can then increase the likelihood that you will be launching with a better fit with what the client is looking for, rather than relying on your own assumptions as to what you think they want. It just increases the chances that you will be offering something they want to buy.

Figure 2.5

Image

One of the issues we need to think about at this stage is what you are going to call your business; what image do you want to portray, a great deal of which can be derived from the name.

I am not a marketer but as I see it you have three options. First is that you go for a derivative of your own name, which is fine; second is that you go for something that gives a very clear indication of what you do, which is also fine; the third one, which is particularly relevant if you anticipate doing more than one activity, is to go for a neutral name, so you can do multiple activities under one identity without unduly confusing anyone.

Students of political history will not be surprised that I did not call my company David Mellor and Co. or David Mellor and Partners. I was also unsure even then whether I would be undertaking a single or multiple activities.

So, I went for a neutral name, Primovant. It was medieval English for what astronomers considered to be the centre of the universe, so there were no ego issues involved at all! It no longer exists as when Stephen Furner and I agreed to set up what is now Viridian it was no longer required – more on that later in the book.

If you are going to go down the incorporation route (we will come back to that shortly), just check that the name is available so that you don't waste time or money on a name you can't use, and also check that the URL is available because you will get very frustrated if you get caught up in design work only to find that you can't register either the company or the URL. Both are easy to do.

If you are going to be a sole trader, just check your local Yellow Pages and make sure there is no one else trading under the same name. Obviously don't "take the Mickey" and call yourself a well know brand!

If you are going to have a logo, please check what it looks like when it is photocopied or faxed. Some things look great in colour but rubbish in "black and white" and you can't read them, so do the black and white test.

Finally before we move on, please make sure that you don't fall foul of the Disability Discrimination Act; there are certain colours which are not friendly to those with visual impairment, so you have to make sure that whatever you have on your website is in colours that people who are partially sighted can read. Whoever you use to create your website should be aware of this.

Strategic Plan

I always describe the planning process as a journey. Imagine you were going to the South of France on holiday; once you have identified the resort the next thing you would do, assuming you were going to be driving, is to plan your route. Why treat your business any differently? A strategic plan is your destination, what you want the company to look like and stand for. Think back to the Nelson Mandela story. Can you imagine what your business is going to look like in three years time? The business plan is your operational map and route to get you there. It has often been said that "Nobody plans to fail but many people fail to plan". "Storming Norman" of Desert Storm fame reportedly said that a good plan today is better than a perfect plan tomorrow, so just get on and do it! The following quote I saw framed in the office of one of my clients: "The nice thing about not planning is that failure comes as a complete and utter surprise and is not proceeded by long periods of worry, anguish and self-doubt". My favourite quote is an old Chinese saying, "A sailor who embarks without a destination cannot possibly hope for a favourable wind". If you do not have a plan, how do you know what you are aiming for? Planning is important then!

VBS Business Plan
Strategy

- Vision – "Achieving Growth through Trust"

- Core Business – providing virtual support to the SME market

- Business Objective – to be the trusted provider of choice...

- Business Strategy – by building trusted relationships and exceeding client expectations

- Key Success Factor – maximising networks

Figure 2.6

I have decided to take as an example someone whose core business is going to be providing virtual operational support to the small and medium sized business (SME) market. Imagine for the moment that this could be you, and it might help you appreciate how a plan could be put together to start such a business.

On the facing page (Figure 2.6) I have set out the "Strategy" part of a "one-page plan". Imagine you are going to set-up a business providing operational support to small businesses. Let's call it Virtual Business Support (VBS) Ltd. The vision is that you are going to grow your business through trust. It is all about buying trust, which is in short stock at the moment! We are going to make you trusted. You are going to get your clients to trust you, and that is the value and principle which you are going to live out in your business and which is going to be the bedrock of your strategy.

Your core business is going to be simple. You are not going to get distracted by anything else. Your business objective is to be the trusted supplier of choice; if people have an operational problem, they think of you first. Your business strategy is that you are going to build trusted relationships and exceed clients' expectations not just meet them. Finally the key success factor is to maximise your network, both existing

and planned (more on that later). Not more complicated than that.

Business Plan

There are a vast number of templates available to you which are all pretty much variations on a theme. You could well find that the one-pager which I suggested, and which we are building, may be sufficient for your initial purposes. If however you need to go to a bank or an investor then you may need more; if you can answer the 10 questions on the following page (Figure 2.7) in robust fashion then you are in pretty good shape. You may have to tweak the questions a little to fit your business but if you can answer them all in confident fashion you are well placed to proceed.

I reckon I have looked at over 5,000 business plans over the last 10 years from a fundraising perspective. A few pages overleaf (Figure 2.8) are the main reasons why they were not progressed by lenders or investors. A few comments on these.

- Lifestyle versus value business - we talked about this earlier. Remember, banks and investors do not see it as their job to fund your lifestyle!

Key Questions A Business Plan Should Address

- *Where is the company today?*

- *What is the product or service?*

- *What is the market/sector?*

- *How will the market be reached?*

- *Who is the competition (today and tomorrow)?*

- *How will the product be produced?*

- *Who are the people?*

- *What are the financial projections?*

- *How much funding is required?*

- *What are the risks?*

Figure 2.7

- Unbalanced team with key skills gaps - unless your plan indicates how you propose to address this, financial backers will be nervous. Unclear product proposition - if you do not make it easy for the reader to grasp your proposition, he or she will quickly lose interest. Remember to avoid jargon!
- Limited analysis of competition - if you put in your business plan that you have no competition your plan will go straight to the discard pile; - people will either believe a) that you are lazy or b) that if there is no competition there is probably no market.
- Unproven revenue model - this is difficult if you are a pre-revenue start-up. How can you prove how much you can sell at what price and with what kind of frequency unless you have done the type of research the florist did.
- Incomplete sales plan - you need to give the reader a clear indication as to how you are going to reach the people who will buy from you. If you mention your route to market, your sales qualification process, your pipeline management process, and your activity and conversion ratio model, you will make them comfortable (see Chapter 3).
- No sensitivity analysis - it is helpful if you do a best case, middle case and worst case,

Typical Shortcomings in a Business Plan

- _No clear understanding re 'lifestyle' or 'value' approach_

- _Unbalanced team with key skill gaps_

- _Unclear product proposition_

- _Limited analysis of competition_

- _Unproven revenue model_

- _Incomplete sales plan_

- _No sensitivity analysis_

- _Limited attention to audience (repayment for lender, return for investor)_

Figure 2.8

so that the reader has an idea of how your financial model looks in different scenarios.

- Attention to audience - if you are talking to a bank their main interest is your ability to service the debt and pay them back; if you are talking to investors, their interest is your ability to give them a higher return than they can get from any other project, or from the stock market.

Back to our one-pager, we can complete the Marketing and Sales part (Figure 2.9 on the following page). We have talked about the pitch, and a little bit about the website. The details behind sales qualification process, pipeline process, and conversion ratio process will become clear when we have covered sales in Chapter 3.

VBS Business Plan
Marketing and Sales

- *Simple but compelling pitch*

- *Dynamic website with supporting collateral*

- *Sales qualification process*

- *Pipeline process*

- *Conversion ratio process*

Figure 2.9

Operations

We are now on to Operations; how are we going to structure and run this business. I am grateful to my Accountant David Beckman who created the table on page 110 (Figure 2.10) which I trust is largely self-explanatory.

The most popular choice is between sole trader and limited company. This is an area where it makes sense to take professional advice, but there are three reasons why, from the layman's point of view, incorporation needs to be seriously considered. One is legal, one is commercial, and one is financial. The legal reason is all around limited liability, as per David's table. If you set up a company, then it is the company that has the trading relationship with your client, and not you. If for any reason something went wrong and the client, or anyone else for that matter, came after you seeking compensation, the risk would generally be limited to the company's ability to pay, unless you had been criminal or fraudulent in your activity, or had given a personal guarantee. If you are a sole trader then your entire personal wealth is on the line, including house, savings etc. The commercial reason why I think it makes sense is the fact that unless you are offering a traditional "trade" e.g. electrician, carpenter, plumber or gardener, having a corporate structure may make you more likely

to look more credible in the eyes of the potential client; furthermore you may not otherwise be able to obtain access to approved or preferred supplier lists now favoured by many businesses.

The third reason is that, despite Government tinkering, there is still a very marginal tax advantage in being incorporated rather than being a sole trader. I think in reality this is outweighed by the commercial and legal reasons, but this is my own personal opinion; please talk to an accountant or lawyer.

If you opt for the sole trader structure, you just need to open a "number two" account at your bank set up in your trading name.

If you go down the corporate route, you will need to open a company bank account, which you can't do until you have a Certificate of Incorporation and Memorandum of Articles of Association. In terms of Incorporation you have three options. In order of cost you can do it yourself (and the Companies House website is very user friendly), you can pay a company formation company to do it for you, or you can get your accountant or lawyer to do it for you.

Legal Entity	Forming	East of Running	Cost of Running	Extracting Funds	Possible Liabilities
Sole Trader	Easy and Cheap	Relatively Easy	Quite cheap £250 to £450	Relatively easy	Unlimited liability
Partnership (Psp)	Quite Easy Quite Cheap Psp Agreement	Relatively easy	More expensive than Sole Trader £450 to £750	Relatively easy	Unlimited liability – joint & several liability
Limited Company	Costs More £150 - £425 Formalities Ownership versus Management	Formalities e.g. board minutes, resolutions, meetings, Annual Returns, Notepaper	More expensive than sole trader or psp £750 to £1,500	Salary or dividend	Possibly limited – but watch for personal guarantees
Limited Liability Partnership (LLP)	Needs to be registered at Companies House	Like a Psp but also needs Annual Returns and minutes	Slightly more expensive than a	Similar to a partnership Tax higher for a	Limits the liability of members – can keep cars within

SOLE TRADER, PARTNERSHIP OR LIMITED COMPANY

Figure 2.10

There are five basic legs to your supporting infrastructure, and they are:

1. Finance
2. Legal
3. Insurance
4. IT
5. HR

I am indebted to five of my closest associates who have each prepared a "top tips" list for you which you will find in the appendix section at the end of this book. These five areas, together with marketing and sales, will be where you incur costs.

We can now complete the Operations part of our one-page plan. Please see figure 2.11 on the following page. We will have a business structure (or if the business is just you will allocate your time) based on the cornerstone principles which you learnt about earlier in this book. We will have robust documentation. We will have a simple but effective CRM system to keep track of your clients and prospects. We will have a delivery process to maximise repeat business and get referrals from satisfied clients. We will have a culture of quality control, with regular client reviews and business improvement reviews.

VBS Business Plan
Operations

- Business structure based on 'cornerstones' principles

- Robust contractual documentation

- Simple but effective CRM (client relationship management) system

- Delivery Process to maximise repeat business and quality referrals

- Culture of quality control (client reviews and business improvement reviews)

Figure 2.11

VBS Business Plan
Finance

- *16 billable days per month (by year-end)*

- *Rate average of £250 per day*

- *No dilution by external associates so 100% gross profit*

- *Total costs to be contained at 20% of turnover*

- *Lifestyle business*

Figure 2.12

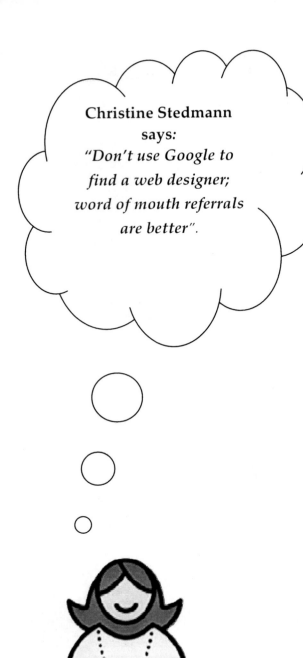

Financial Plan

We are also in a position to complete the finance part of our one-page plan (figure 2.12). Please view the numbers as for illustrative purposes only. What I have assumed (for you!) is that by the year end, your run rate will be 16 billable days work per month, so pretty full! You are working on an average rate of £250 per day. You are not diluting your income by using anyone else. You are going to be stringent on costs, and you are going to keep your costs at 20% of turnover; and finally, whilst you will "upgrade" to a value business in due course, you are in Year 1 going to organise your net earnings to support yourself and if applicable the family.

Over the next few pages are forecasts for profit and loss and cash flow that reflect this. (Figure 2.13 and Figure 2.14).

Profit and Loss Forecast

Figure 2.13

	JAN	FEB	MAR	APR	MAY	JUN	JUL	AUG	SEP	OCT	NOV	DEC	TOT
Sales	1,000	1,000	1,000	2,000	2,000	2,000	3,000	3,000	3,000	4,000	4,000	4,000	30,000
Cost of Sales	0	0	0	0	0	0	0	0	0	0	0	0	0
Gross Profit	1,000	1,000	1,000	2,000	2,000	2,000	3,000	3,000	3,000	4,000	4,000	4,000	30,000
Overhead	200	200	200	400	400	400	600	600	600	800	800	800	6,000
Net Profit	800	800	800	1,600	1,600	1,600	2,400	2,400	2,400	3,200	3,200	3,200	24,000
Reserve	200	200	200	400	400	400	600	600	600	800	800	800	6,000
Dividend	600	600	600	1,200	1,200	1,200	1,800	1,800	1,800	2,400	2,400	2,400	18,000

Assumptions

- As per the one-page plan
- Reserve (25%) established to ensure business stays cash positive and tax liabilities can be met as they fall due.
- VAT ignored
- No allowance for set-up (as opposed to maintenance) costs e.g. pc, laptop, printer, website
- All costs re Marketing and Sales and Infrastructure included as overhead

Cash Flow Forecast
Figure 2.14

	JAN	FEB	MAR	APR	MAY	JUN	JUL	AUG	SEP	OCT	NOV	DEC
Cash b/f	1,000	1,000	1,200	1,400	1,600	2,000	2,400	2,800	3,400	4,000	4,600	5,400
Sales	0	1,000	1,000	1,000	2,000	2,000	2,000	3,000	3,000	3,000	4,000	4,000
Total cash	1,000	2,000	2,200	2,400	3,600	4,000	4,400	5,800	6,400	7,000	8,600	9,400
Overhead	0	200	200	200	400	400	400	600	600	600	800	800
Net Cash	1,000	1,800	2,000	2,200	3,200	3,600	4,000	5,200	5,800	6,400	7,800	8,600
Dividend	0	600	600	600	1,200	1,200	1,200	1,800	1,800	1,800	2,400	2,400
Cash c/f	1,000	1,200	1,400	1,600	2,000	2,400	2,800	3,400	4,000	4,600	5,400	6,200

Assumptions

- £1,000 put in as opening capital
- Dividend paid 1 month in arrears
- All debtors pay 1 month in arrears
- All creditors paid one month in arrears
- All per the one-page plan
- Reserve (25%) established to ensure business stays cash positive and tax liabilities can be met as they fall due
- VAT ignored
- No allowance for set-up (as opposed to maintenance) costs e.g. pc, laptop, printer, website
- All costs re Marketing and Sales and Infrastructure included as overhead

Funding Strategy

If you need external finance to launch your business, then realistically you have three main options, in addition to any government grants or funding schemes which are specific to your locality (your local Business Link is the best place to research this).

1. "FFF" - This is short for Founders, Family, and Friends. This represents the logical starting point.
2. The Banks - The government introduced a new scheme in 2008 to stimulate lending to small businesses, which has a partial government guarantee. If for any reason you are not eligible for this scheme (known as the Enterprise Finance Guarantee or EFG Scheme), you will probably have to provide security (e.g. guarantee probably supported by a mortgage over your home) to obtain either working capital finance or asset finance.
3. The business angel community - there will be one or more business angel communities in your locality, as they do not usually like to be more than 2 hours away from their investments.

On the following pages I have set out my top tips on dealing with banks and angels respectively (Figure 2.15 and Figure 2.16).

Top Tips for Dealing With Banks

- _You need to prove your ability to service the debt (plus interest) with something to spare_

- _They will be looking for security when lending to young businesses_

- _They will fund assets and working capital_

- _They will very rarely fund people and salaries_

- _They will have concerns re risk and reward_

Figure 2.15

Top Tips for Dealing With Investors

- Exit Strategy is often their No. 1 priority

- Return on investment is critical

- They will be looking closely at the potential of your business

- They will also look closely at the management

- They will not fund the owners' lifestyle

Figure 2.16

Why Small Businesses Fail

If I put my black hat on and talk about the main reasons that small businesses fail, it's not because I want to depress you just at the point of launching, it's mainly to tell you where the traps are so that you can avoid them.

Small businesses fail because they run out of cash; and we already know that probably the biggest reason that this happens is because they did not fully understand what they were getting into. But there are other reasons that can come into play:

- Lack of self-awareness - they have been unrealistic about their strengths and weaknesses, i.e. they thought they were good at sales when they were not. I can think of somebody down in Sussex who thought they were the best thing since sliced bread in terms of sales but they were selling at the wrong price which meant the more business they did, the more money they lost
- Research - they came up with a product or a service which was a solution looking for a problem; their research was insufficient for them to clarify that there was a market for what they wanted to do.

- Underestimating costs - you should be able to figure out your costs; don't guess for example what your insurance costs will be - find out. If you use as many real numbers as possible, you can then figure out what your breakeven point is, and then you know how much money you have to make to cover your costs before you start making money.

- Allowing customers too long to pay - if you talk to any owner of a small business and ask them what their biggest gripe is, number one is almost always bad debts. If your model is business to consumer, and you are dealing with the public, it is slightly different; by and large you will be paid by cash or cheque or credit card so you are safeguarded to a certain extent, and also the timeline is shorter. If however you are doing business to business it is a different game. If your clients are other small businesses you will need to be careful. Some of them will try every trick in the book to delay paying you. It is amazing how creative other businesses can be. If your terms and conditions say you want payment in 30 days do not believe that they are making every conceivable effort to comply, because they probably are not! If you think they are, then you are potentially deluded.

If on the other hand your clients are going to be big companies then you still need to be vigilant, as they are quite often inefficient in terms of paying product and service providers. They are not paying you because they don't want to, they are not paying you because they can't find the invoice, they can't match it to the transaction, or they have paid someone else. One of my clients is a software company who sell to large companies. The husband does the selling and delivery, and the wife does the bookkeeping and invoicing. She is on first name terms with at least two people in the accounts payable department of their clients. She knows whose tray the invoice has to be in and by what date to hit the next payables run. From time to time she will send them tickets to the theatre, or a case of wine, to say thank you for their ongoing business and prompt payment; they have never had a bad debt in 18 years, and their days sales outstanding is as low as you can possibly get it. But it is time consuming.

One of the small business consultancies where I used to be actively involved has a secret weapon in the form of their book keeper, who also does the invoicing.

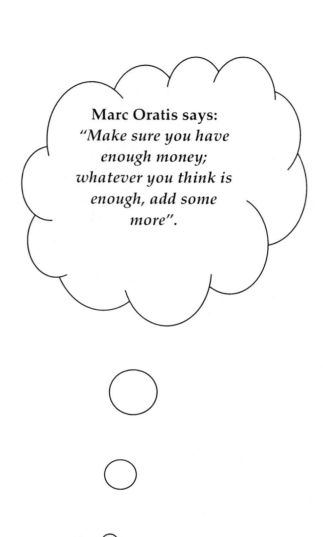

If you assume that all the invoices from the previous month are going out on the first of the next month, then this is easier to follow. So let's assume that the next wave of invoices is going out 1st October. On the 30th September she will call each of the clients, advise them that the invoices are being done, and then check that the amount in question is what they are expecting. The reason she does this is to prevent a situation where after several weeks silence they are chased and then claim that it was not what they were expecting. So, she is taking away the ability for them to play the "not what I was expecting" card. Having sent the invoices, she will then telephone to check that they have been received, which takes away the "never received it" card. She does both of those in the immediate timescale of the invoice going out and as it gets closer to the contractual payment date (30 days) she is all over them for payment. That is the way that you have to do it if you are a small business but it is time consuming. Don't assume that people will pay you, or pay you in a timely fashion, if you have done the work.

- Insufficient due diligence - my first client became a bad debt. The lead came through the head of sales of one of the companies where I was a Non Executive Director whilst at Deutsche Bank. I launched in to help and I did not ask the right questions, or listen properly because of the route it reached me; not only did I not get paid, I did not get my expenses reimbursed - the company traded in New York: the founder of the client company disappeared to Africa, never to be seen again, leaving a huge trail of creditors, of whom I was a tiny one. The people who put me in touch with him were mortified (they were owed much more money than me) that they had put me in that position; but ultimately it was my fault; I just should have done my own investigations. If I did it again I would have asked to see his financial figures to see if he had an ability to pay. The guy was a smooth operator; it's easy to get duped: I was keen to get my first piece of business and it was a harsh lesson to learn.

- "Registered Charity Syndrome" – this is where people wittingly or unwittingly try to separate you from what you know without paying for it. An example from my world of the "unwitting" is one of my early clients.

When I first started working with him, his business was much smaller than it is now and we had a different financial arrangement; he was forever phoning me or emailing me, saying, for example that he had just agreed a strategic alliance and could I look over the heads of terms before it went to the lawyers, or he was drafting an advert/job specification for a new member of staff and could I review it. I worked out one month I had done over a day's work in bits and pieces that I had not been paid for. It is so easy to end up doing this; when I told him, he was surprised and shocked and so we changed our arrangement and I moved on to a retainer basis which would cover ad-hoc email and telephone support.

The other type is "witting" i.e. where somebody knowingly does it. As you know, I have a business partner called Stephen and we met way back in 2002; in our first year I was approached by a South African gentleman who was finance director of a property company; he was looking to raise half a million pounds for a transaction, and we were recommended to him. I met him and we chatted for an hour or so; I then created a proposal, sent it to him and he thought it was great. He asked to meet again to ask some questions before he put it to the board and so I went and met him again.

He said it was a lot of money if he signed up with us and he wanted to know what he would get for his money, so I explained what we would be doing and he said he would put it to his board. I then went off to the States leaving Stephen to deal with any queries from the board. Sure enough this guy came back to Stephen saying that there were questions from the board, which Stephen duly answered. We had now spent five (unremunerated) hours with him and never heard from him again. Stupidly we had told him everything he needed to know to go and do the job himself. He did not need us. That is what I mean by the registered charity syndrome; there will be people out there that who will try to take advantage of you. There is a fine line between how much you have to tell them to satisfy them without giving away your "crown jewels" of wisdom that you have spent years acquiring. People will try and trick you into giving away information. Be aware of it.

Finally, choosing the wrong business partners - most business partnerships do not work. It's not because people are bad; it's mainly because circumstances change. If you take a simple example of two people who decide that they are going to work together. On the day they agree to start they are both 100% on the same page, but sooner or later one of them will drift and once the drift starts it is very hard to reverse the process.

That drift could be caused by something more exciting coming along for one of them, their priorities changing, a health scare, or a family issue of some sort. I have seen all of these happen. Unless you put in place a mechanism to deal with changing circumstances when you start, you will begin to see resentment, as one party senses that the commitment and effort are not balanced anymore.

I can think of two examples from my world. I was doing a strategic workshop with a small consultancy run by a man and a woman, who operated a partnership with a group of about 12 associates. They had been going for about three years and doing very well. They had an idea for a big new venture which was going to be capital intensive and they wanted to be put through an intensive "stress test"; the purpose was to see that if they went to the bank/business angel community they would be taken seriously. They wanted the assurance that their new business idea made sense, and that their existing business was in good shape. The woman was doing most of the delivery and the man was the ambassador creating the awareness and lining up the prospects. One of the issues I usually try to establish is how people allocate their time.

The lady was "on fees" doing client work pretty much full time , so it was clear what she was doing, but he was not doing a lot that was fee related; I was thinking that there was only a finite amount of networking and prospecting that he could be doing each week, so what was he actually doing? I kept trying to explore how he spent his time, but he was resistant; mid afternoon, however, it came out.

All the time she thought he was out there marketing and prospecting for the partnership he was doing something completely different. The man had recently married, and whilst his business partner was out there bringing the money in, he was helping his new wife set up a restaurant business. You could have heard a pin drop. When they had both calmed down we had a very difficult conversation about the next steps. I had a long depressing drive home but two days later I received a letter and a cheque for the work. She said it was the best day's consultancy she had ever experienced, and she did not know how many years of deception I had managed to short circuit. I have no doubt that on the day they set their partnership up they were both 100% matched, but his priorities changed and it is hard to imagine a situation where they could get back to a genuine partnership of equals. The partnership was dissolved within three months.

If I contrast this unhappy tale with my working relationship with Stephen. As I have already mentioned Stephen and I met in 2002; we are very different in terms of the way we work, and indeed the work we do, but the arrangement is very successful. One of the key aspects I think is that we see eye to eye on the issues that matter; we have never had a cross word in seven years! When we met - and we met through networking - we saw opportunities to work together. What we did, without involving any lawyers, was draft out one page of A4 with some basic but important terms of reference, detailing how we were going to work, what we were going to call ourselves, what kind of business we were going to look for, our pricing model, the amount of money we were going to invest, and the amount of time we were going to commit. After 12 months we planned to take stock and then decide what next. Well, during that first year I think we made a small profit, which was not bad in view of the market conditions. During that year we were lied to, cheated, played off against each other; we also encountered the

South African finance director I mentioned and so the year was not without its excitement.

We sat down and had a beer at the end of the year and we decided you learn more about people during adversity than when things are going well. So we set the company up and away we went.

A postscript to this story though – we eventually experienced the drift... but it was me, not Stephen. I heard the siren call of doing other interesting work, and became set on developing a portfolio career, whereas Stephen was still channelling all his effort and energy into the company. I raised the subject before any resentment could set in. So what we did was adjust the shareholding from 50-50 so that Stephen became the majority shareholder, which reflected this change in circumstance. The way we went about it was adult, professional and it made sense! We were still aligned but in a way that better reflected our respective levels of commitment. You could imagine how, if that conversation had not taken place, there could have been resentment.

So if you are going into partnership with someone else, be very careful of how you set it up, why you are setting it up and how you will deal with it if it does not go according to plan.

SELF-DIAGNOSTIC TWO
Are you finished with your planning phase?

NO	ISSUE	SCORE out of 10
1	Have you completed a business skills inventory?	
2	Have you worked out a training/resourcing plan based on the inventory?	
3	Have you defined what success will look like for you?	
4	Have you fully researched the market?	
5	Have you created some basic sales and delivery processes?	
6	Have you established your cost base?	
7	Do you have a revenue model?	
8	Have you identified a mentor?	
9	Have you profiled your clients?	
10	Have you identified and analysed your competition?	
TOTAL		

Score < 30   *You may be embarking on your business "eyes wide shut"! More homework may be required.*

Score < 60   *You may want to spend some more time preparing for launch*

Score > 60   *You probably have enough momentum to proceed to the launch phase.*

SELF DIAGNOSTIC TWO

You are now ready to take the second test (facing page) – are you done with planning?

CHAPTER 3
Doing....

Awareness

- *Word of mouth*

- *Launch party*

- *Flyers*

- *Press Release*

- *Promotional Offer*

- *Trade show/exhibition*

- *Advertising*

- *Business Cards*

- *Traditional Networking*

- *Website*

- *Brochures*

- *Social Networking – e.g. LinkedIn*

- *Promotional Gift or Gadget*

- *Direct Marketing (mail, e-mail, telephone)*

Figure 3.1

CHAPTER 3
Doing...

Awareness

Today is "Launch Day" - you have opened for business today, but no one out there knows you exist. So what are you going to do to let them know? What you can do probably depends on what your business is, but will be a "cocktail" of the list on the facing page (Figure 3.1). Networking is so important it will have its own section shortly.

And a few words on website. Five years ago I would have said that a website was a "nice to have" on launch day, as opposed to a "need to have". Things have moved on and if you are going to be taken seriously you really need one, however minimalist. There are two reasons. Firstly, if you launch your business and don't have a website you run the risk that your potential clients will question your seriousness. Secondly, increasingly it is becoming the icebreaker conversation if you are meeting somebody new. If I meet somebody at a networking event, and we agree to meet up at a later date, the opening conversation at the subsequent meeting often relates to the website. If you don't have one you take away the icebreaker conversation.

Routes to Market

You should have more than one of these. The obvious route to market is people who will buy direct from you. The second route to market is people who will refer prospects to you, in the expectation that you will do the same for them. The third route is people who would be prepared to sell on your behalf, i.e. they would introduce clients to you but they would expect to be paid in some way. The fourth route is people who do something that is either similar to you or complementary to you, with the result that that you can sell alongside them and the two of you can win business together that you could not win on your own. You each help the other.

And finally, the fifth route is networks that you could join with the specific purpose of building relationships and promoting your business. This would be the biggest change for most people but it could also well be your biggest source of business. Which takes us on to networking...

MARKETING MIX

Figure 3.2

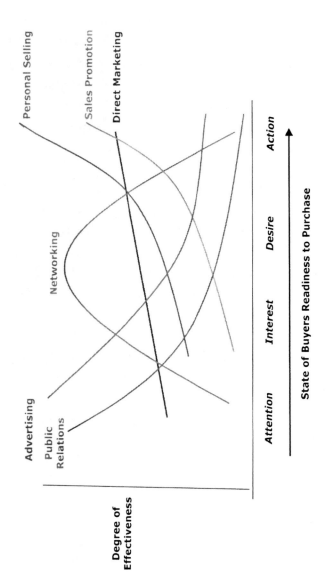

Networking

My starting point for this very important topic is the diagram on the facing page (figure 3.2) – the value of a marketing mix. I have seen this diagram so often that I cannot recall when I first encountered it. It is the best diagrammatic summary of the marketing mix I have seen. It is based on a state of mind called AIDA which represents the different stage of readiness of a buyer to buy. AIDA (in the "x" axis) stands for Attention, Interest, Desire and Action. Apparently what happens is, something catches your attention, it arouses your interest, it creates a desire for you to buy, but you still have to take action. At any of those four stages you can "drop off". That is the buying process. If you are buying a book it could be a matter of seconds; if it is an item of clothing, it could be hours, if its furniture it could be days, a car could be weeks, a house could be years.

What the "y" axis tells you is the degree of effectiveness of different types of marketing. Having understood this you can now go away and figure out what would be the marketing "cocktail" for your business that would give you the optimal result.

If you look at Advertising and PR they are fantastic at getting people's attention; they will

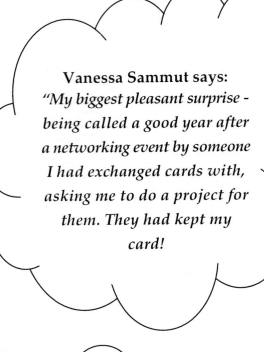

Vanessa Sammut says:
"My biggest pleasant surprise - being called a good year after a networking event by someone I had exchanged cards with, asking me to do a project for them. They had kept my card!

create some interest but if nothing else happens, interest will dwindle away; you may get some sales from them but not many. If you look at Direct Marketing (telesales, mailshots, e-broadcasts ...), what that is telling you is that it will capitalise on the attention you have managed to generate and you will get some sales but again not many - the typical return on a direct marketing campaign is 1%. It's very much a numbers game.

The Sales Promotion line tells us that we can build on any attention that we have created by special offers, and generate some sales.

You will also see that, in most cases, there is no substitute for Personal Sales i.e. face-to-face selling.

I have deliberately left until last the "hump" represented by Networking; you will see that this is very much the "glue" that holds everything else together. So Networking is a completely different activity from selling. Networking is building relationships with people who will do one of two things: they will either buy from you when they are ready or they know people whom they can refer to you who might buy from you. It's all about building relationships until such time as you can intervene with a personal sale and win the business. That is why networking is so important but so often underestimated and/or misused. Think about it for a moment: if you are

talking to somebody at a networking event the likelihood that they are in the market at that moment in time for what you do is not high, which is why this process is so important.

The obvious place to start is your existing network of family, friends, neighbours and people who you have worked with in your career thus far. What I suggest you do is collect all the names on an excel spreadsheet (particularly the work contacts) and classify them 1 – 5.

1. People you are convinced will buy from you at some stage in the future
2. People you are pretty certain will buy from you but you are not quite so sure
3. People who realistically are never going to buy from you but you like them, they are well networked, and they are useful for market intelligence
4. People where you really have no idea whether they are potential buyers or not
5. People you consider to be irrelevant in your new world.

Having numbered them, you can immediately archive the 5s; the 4s and the 2s you create a diary system to be in touch with them every other month; the 3s you do the same but on a quarterly basis; and the 1s you find a reason to be in touch once a month without irritating them. By the

Vanessa Sammut says:
"Have an income to fall back on in the early months; you won't have a full portfolio of clients on day one. Don't underestimate the power of networking, you are the product and explaining what you do face to face is the best way of generating business, even if you hate doing it!

end of Year 1, you should only have 1s and 3s left. The 2s will become 1, 3 or 5s, same with the 4s. The 5s have already been archived. You can still be reactive toward the 5s, but you cannot afford to spend time on them; you have to spend time on those who are the most relevant. You also need to have enough time to add new and highly relevant people to your network. There is nothing to stop you getting on and doing this now! You don't have to wait as you know who they are.

The second type of networking is opportunistic. You go to an event, an exhibition, or a trade fair, where you will have opportunities to "work the room". You can talk to people - at registration, and in the breaks. If you attend an event that is relevant to your business, in that room could be potential clients, competitors, potential service providers to you and people you can team up with. I have not gone to an event where I have not come away with at least two or three cards of people to follow up with, however good or bad the event was.

The third category is planned networking. This is where you join a networking group for the specific purpose of building relationships and promoting your business. The only one I have time to do now is CADIA (www.cadia.org.uk) which meets once a month. The website will

David Mellor - Elevator Pitch

Good morning everyone, my name is David Mellor from Viridian Corporate Finance, based in the Gatwick Area. What do we do? We help business owners make more money and free up their time. How do we do that? We take them out of their natural habitat, we help them review where their business is, identify where they would like to take it, but most importantly we work alongside them for as long as it takes to help them get there. Benefits for them are that it puts them back in control of their business, and it gives them a direction and a focus, all of which lead to increased profitability. Typical issues that we find are that they are working far too many hours, they are not making enough money, they don't trust any of their staff to do the job as well as they can and quite often they are lonely. So if you know any business owners that show any of those symptoms, I would love to hear from them; just remember my name is David Mellor from Viridian in the Gatwick area - you have my contact details on my card. Oh and don't forget - you don't want to end up like Christopher Columbus, who when he set off did not know where he was going, when he got there he did not know where he was, and when he got back he did not know where he had been. He did it all with somebody else's money, but you probably don't have that luxury. Thank you.

Figure 3.3

give you a pretty good idea of what an organised networking group is all about. Other networking groups are run by Chambers of Commerce, BNI and the IOD. For the ladies there is one which is called "Women in Business". It's worth going along as a guest/visitor to a few events to gauge which ones suit you best. Once you have made a decision you will need to stick at it though, as it takes time to build trusted relationships.

They are all variations on a theme, and generally give you an opportunity to tell your story to either your table, or the full group, depending on how many attendees there are. This usually takes the form of an "elevator pitch". An example of what I might say is on the facing page (Figure 3.3).

In an elevator pitch you tell people who you are, where you are based, what your business is, what you do, what makes you different, the kind of clients you are looking for, a reminder of how to contact you and finally some kind of memory hook or strap line which makes you memorable - in my case the Columbus story!

If you remember five things about networking, make it the following:

1. It is not about selling, but all about building relationships.
2. The most you can realistically achieve is a

Our interviews showed that the Top 3 "Pleasant Surprises" were:

1. Winning first customer

2. Proving to yourself you can do it

3. Finding that there are a lot of helpful and supportive people out there

follow-up meeting to find out more about their business. I stress to find out about their business rather than tell them about yours (that comes later).

3. If you do come across somebody that you can help, (or when you know somebody else who can help them) make sure you follow-up.

4. Be prepared to talk to people you don't know - don't just stick to the people you do know.

5. Stick at it - persistence pays and remember if you do things for other people they will be more motivated to do things for you.

Sales

The next key component is sales. When I run my workshops I do a little word association exercise; I say one word and ask the delegates to write down the first thing that comes into their head.

The one word is "Salesperson" - the responses I generally receive are predominately negative, including words such as:

- Impolite
- Shallow
- Pushy
- Smoothie

- Aggressive
- Shark
- Bully
- Suit
- Sleazy
- Scumbag

It is fair to say that most of the words volunteered are not words that you would feel happy being used about yourself!

So, ladies and gentlemen, we have a challenge; if we are going to eat then normally we have to sell and yet we associate selling with pushy, sleazy scumbags in suits! So how do we do sales without having to risk ourselves being perceived as one or more of the negative images conjured up? I have to try to demystify the sales process for you and make it slightly less scary.

My personal view is there are three attributes of a successful salesperson:

1. The first attribute is the ability to be liked. If you consider your own experience, you are more likely to buy from somebody you like!

2. The second attribute is the ability to listen. There is a famous saying that God gave us two ears and one mouth and we should use them in that proportion, and this is

Norman Burnham says:
"If you believe in yourself, your product, your customer, then do not let others stand in your way. Always take advice and ask for help, it is not often refused. Do not be arrogant, learn to listen".

absolutely true. The good salesperson asks the right questions then shuts up, and if you have asked the right questions and remain silent the client will tell you all you need to know. Some of the best salespeople I have encountered are amongst the quietest people I know.

3. The third one is to my mind the hardest one to handle, namely the ability to enter the client's world, rather than try to drag the client into yours. That is where most people fall down.

When people get into the sales process and are in the thick of it, they get nervous and tense. When that happens, they revert to where they are comfortable, namely themselves and their business, and they stop talking about the client and his or her business. What you are trying to do is solve their problem in their world. If you can master that, coupled with the other two attributes, then you have the main components of a good sales person. You still need a process to work with and some tools at your disposal, but in terms of a sound base, you will have it.

Next, let's take a look at some of the things that can happen in sales meetings. Firstly, features and benefits. You really need to appreciate the difference. A feature is what something does; a benefit is what it does for the client. The danger

Our Interviews showed that the Top 3 "Dark Moments" were:

1. Taking time to get going and make money and fear of running out of time and cash

2. Nothing to show for marketing in general and networking in particular for a long time

3. Having to do everything, particularly the admin

is that people tend to focus in client meetings about the features but not benefits, which reduces the number of sales they can get because it is the thing that is of least interest to the client but quite often the most interest to the seller. If you have devised a funky piece of software, you want to tell everyone about it, but the client really does not care; they want to know what it does for them in their world. When I did my sales training they had me selling a car. From memory I had to make the point that it was fitted with halogen headlamps (feature), which meant that it was safer to drive in the dark, (benefit). Bearing in mind if it is a consumer sale the benefit does not have to be a financial one and, in this case, it was safety. I was paired up with the sales trainer who said he was an old man who did not drive at night; so I sold him a benefit that was completely irrelevant to him! But the point was made. If you then apply this to a business to business sale - you can begin to see how it works. Imagine that you have just been appointed the UK head of sales for a company selling "hands-free" phone kits and you are calling on the manager of a big call centre.

You demonstrate the hands-free kit and say that this means that the operatives in the call centre can work completely hands-free, and therefore complete more transactions per day which means

Stuart Hillston says:

"My biggest pleasant surprise – There is generally a point in any new business where you suddenly realise you have "turned a corner" and that happened a while ago. It is a great feeling, and does wonders for your confidence. Mine was when I reached the point of being able to turn down projects that I didn't want to do because I had enough of the ones I wanted to do and reaching that point well before the economic decline had turned".

more money for the business. The key words are "which means" as they link the feature to the benefit. They work every time. You have to talk about the features otherwise you can't have a conversation, but you have to link why that is of benefit to the client. If you think about it, if you are not saying "which means" the client is thinking "so what"? It gets you from features to benefits. Trust it as a technique and it works.

The next one is when somebody says to you, "What is your USP"? It's a horrible question to get, but sooner or later someone will ask you. What makes you different?

Why should I use you? USP in marketing terms is either unique selling point, or unique selling proposition. In today's world I think that if somebody else is prepared to throw money or people at it, most USPs can almost certainly be replicated unless you have a secret formula. I believe the definition of a USP is that it's sustainable, defensible and genuinely unique, but if you look around today's market there are not many products or services that hit those criteria. Nevertheless, if somebody says to you "What is your USP?" you need to have an answer - for most people the USP will be you, something about you and the way you transact business.

Our interviews showed that the Top 3 "Unpleasant Surprises" were:

1. *Bad Debts*

2. *Being let down by other people*

3. *Dealing with Banks*

The third one is fielding the question: "How can you prove you can do what you say you are going to do?" This is a hard one to handle. Ways you can deal with this include:

- Do you have relevant qualifications that are evidence that you can do what you say you can do?
- Can you offer some sort of free trial which will make people comfortable?
- Can you get testimonials and references from either satisfied clients or, to buy you time in the early days, business contacts from your previous employment?

That brings us on nicely to sales methodologies, the first of which is the Sales Qualification Process. On the following page (Figure 3.4) is one used by a former client of mine in the storage business.

The key purposes for this company were:

a. To profile the customers they wanted
b. To weed out any potential bad debts
c. To weed out any potential time wasters

A few remarks on each of the components:

- Source of lead or referral - where did the opportunity come from? Is it from a trusted source, who you know would only pass

Sales Qualification Process

- _Source of lead/referral_

- _Potential size of transaction_

- _Size of company/creditworthiness_

- _Identification of decision-maker_

- _Identification of budget (and timing)_

- _Clarity of requirement_

- _Urgency of requirement_

- _Current provider(s)_

Figure 3.4

you a qualified opportunity, or is it a less trusted resource that may be passing you a problem?

- Potential size of transaction - if it's huge, don't just rub your hands together with delight; think about whether you can actually deliver or whether you would embarrass yourself if you could not cope. If it's tiny, don't decline out of hand; think about whether you are being tested, and if you do a good job will you get something more substantial down the line.

- Size of company - in days gone by the larger the company the more likely they would be there to pay you when you finish the work, but the current economic climate has have indicated this is not necessarily the case. With smaller businesses you may want to check their ability to pay. There are credit checks you can do by using agencies that have access to the same databases that the banks have; they normally do debt recovery also! This is obviously for business to business.

- Identification of decision maker – nothing is more frustrating than pitching to the wrong person. If you have identified the decision maker - great; if not can you positively influence the person who is representing your interests to give a good account of your proposition? Make sure you understand the decision-making process.

| | Pipeline | | |
| | Source: Viridian Corporate Finance Limited | | |
Name	Stage	Contract Size(est)	Value
A	1	100	0
B	2	200	20
C	3	50	10
D	4	150	50
E	5	250	125
F	6	100	75
G	7	100	100
H	1	50	0
I	3	250	50
J	4	100	33
K	5	150	75
L	2	200	20
M	2	50	5
N	4	50	16
		1800	579

Assumptions

1. Prospect = 0%
2. Contact established = 10%
3. Positive meeting = 20%
4. Tender submitted = 30%
5. Negotiations/discussions = 50%
6. Verbal o.k. or email = 75%
7. Purchase order/contract = 100%

Figure 3.5

- Identification of budget - find out if your prospect has a budget. If the prospect has not allocated a budget, then how serious are they?
- Clarity of requirement - are you clear in your mind what the client wants and whether you can deliver it?
- Urgency of requirement - Is this mission critical for them or not? If it's not, then if they get busy could it cease to be important?
- Finally, why are they talking to you? What has prompted them to contact you? Are they serious about getting a quote or are you just there to make up the numbers? If that is the case, you do not want to waste your time if there is no chance to win the business.

If you have gone though the qualification process and are still talking, and neither of you has "deselected" the other, then your prospect is going to be surprised if you don't ask for the business.

You also need to manage your sales pipeline. Take a look at the two tables on the facing page and the following page

The first one (Figure 3.5) is very useful in anticipating your future cash flow. The first column is the prospect. The second column is the stage the relationship has reached. The third column is

Pipeline

Figure 3.6

Prospect	Contact Established	Positive Meeting	Tender Submitted	Negotiations/ Discussions	Verbal OK or email	Purchase o. contrac
A	A1	A2	A3	A4	A5	A6
B	B1	B2	B3	B4	B5	B6
C	C1	C2	C3	C4	C5	
D	D1	D2	D3	D4	D5	
E	E1	E2	E3	E4		
F	F1	F2	F3	F4		
G	G1	G2	G3			
H	H1	H2	H3			
I	I1	I2				
J	J1	J2				
K	K1					
L	L1					
M	M1					
N	N1					
O	O1					
P						
Q						
R						
S						
T						
U						
V						
W						
X						
Y						
Z						

Source: Viridian Corporate Finance Limited

the estimated absolute size of the contract. The fourth column is the discounted "value" of the contract, with the estimated size multiplied by the percentage likelihood that the business is won.

By way of example, prospect I is at stage three, so there is a 20% likelihood that you win the business. The business is estimated to be worth £250, so the discounted value is £50.

Another way of looking at your pipeline is the second table. (figure 3.6). It's the same sort of data re-sorted. It shows you how many names you have at each stage in the sales process, so it's useful to estimate what volume of business is coming towards you from a resourcing standpoint. If overnight everything moved from column five to column six you might think "how I am going to deal with this" as they have all said yes at the same time. You can also pick up on things that are stalling; if something has been in column five for ages you might ask yourself why, and investigate.

The key is how many names can you add to the first column, and how fast can you move them to the far-right column.

Activity Plan/ Conversion Ratios

ACTIONS (1500)

One in Ten

MEETINGS (150)

One in Five

PROPOSALS (30)

One in Three

WINS (10)

Figure 3.7

The final component is an Activity Plan and Conversion Ratio chart (Figure 3.7). What this is assuming is that to hit your sales target for the year you need 10 clients. The subsequent assumptions might be:

You can win one in three proposals, so you have to do 30 proposals; once in every five meetings a prospect will ask you to submit a tender or a proposal, so you have to do 150 meetings; and finally out of every 10 people that you contact one agrees to meet with you. If you then flip it the other way, if you contact 1500 people either at a networking meeting or by phone, letter or email, then 150 will agree to meet you, of which 30 will allow you to submit a proposal, and 10 will be won.

You now have a rough estimate of how hard you have to work to get the number of clients you need. In Year 2 it should be more scientific as you will have a year's data. You will have an idea of how much work you would need to do at the front end to get the requisite number of clients. Please note that these ratios are for illustration only.

The final part of the sales process is asking for the business. Let's start with the "alternative close". If the meeting has gone well, you could use this. In my world a successful sale is typically when somebody agrees to do some kind of workshop, so I might say "would you like to do the workshop in October or November" - it's not cheeky; it's an open question and it does work!

The second option is the "summary close" and this is helpful if you have done more than one meeting and if there is more than one decision maker. I had one situation where there were five directors and three meetings with a different mix of directors at each meeting. At the final meeting I said, "We have had three meetings, you have identified over those meetings half a dozen benefits, so for these six reasons would you like to agree a date to do this?" This time you are risking the answer "no", but by reiterating the benefits message you are reminding them of all the different things that they have told themselves - remember they did not all attend all of the meetings.

The third option is the "assumptive close", where you make the decision for them. The meeting has gone so well you make the decision. I did one meeting on the south coast with a husband and wife team, who ran a very successful engineering company. I had persuaded them that they needed to do the workshop off-site and the husband and wife then had an interesting debate about which pub in the town they should use. One had a romantic view; the other did good real ale. It was fairly obvious that they had already made their buying decision so I said, "why don't we settle on the first Friday in December and you let me know which one of the pubs you have booked", and then left them to it!

The "buy signals" were so strong. You can do that when it is clear they have made the decision; you just need to be brave and make the decision for them.

The fourth option is the "concession close". This is particularly helpful if you are doing design or consultancy work where it's clear you need to give something away to get the business - but trade time not money. If there is nothing tangible that you can throw in you are probably reduced down to some sort of trade and I would always trade time and not money. To keep the maths simple, if somebody says to me "what is this going to cost?" and I say, "it looks like it is a day's work so that is £1,000" they might respond: "I did not expect to pay that much", so I might respond "Let's have a look at the seven parts to this job; we could defer a couple of these to another day, one you could do yourself, so if we work hard on the other four parts we could get it done in a half day, so that would be £500". They might say they agree to that. I have not

Stuart Hillston says:
"Ensure you have sufficient resources (money) to survive a year without income – you may not need it, but it will prevent you getting dragged down by cash constraints. And make sure your partner is fully committed too – they will carry as much burden as you".

given it away; I have traded time for money. The worst thing I could have done is say that I would do the whole day for £500 because that devalues me in their eyes. Try to find out if trading time for money works; it often does, particularly if you have pitched in a modular format where you can take components out of your solution.

One situation you may face is where they say they will think it over, which often is a polite way of saying no. If someone says this to you, there is not much you can do, but what you can try is to say: "That's fine. I understand you want to think it over because it is a big decision; just tell me before I go if there is any aspect of what I have told you that needs clarifying, so that you can think it over properly; I would hate you to be under any misapprehension, or worry". Sometimes they tell you, sometimes not. If they do tell you, this is an opportunity to get back on track and complete the sale. If you cannot close the sale, you will need to do further follow-up. Sometimes this will be successful, sometimes not! We use the "rule of seven" approach. If after six attempts to contact the prospect we have had no joy (i.e. calls/emails not returned) our seventh action is to close off the file. We will write and state that we have tried without success to contact on a number of occasions with no success; we will add that we do not wish to irritate them, and appreciate that their priorities and needs

Our interviews showed that when asked "Are you financially better off or matching your previous income" the response was:

Yes -	70%
No -	15%
Maybe -	15%

may have changed; they know who we are, where we are, and what we do, and are welcome to contact us at any time. We stay in control.

Finally, there is the "Jim close". I used to work with Jim in New York and he had the reputation of being one of the top software salesmen on the Eastern Seaboard. If anybody remembers the original Miami Vice, Jim was a dead ringer for Ricardo Tubbs; he dressed like him, walked like him and talked like him - he was very smooth! We did some calls together. When Jim felt the meeting had lasted long enough he would steeple his fingers, lean forward, using body language to draw everyone in, and then lower his voice. He would then indicate that he felt that we had taken the discussion as far as we could and that there was just one thing he needed to know before he left - was there any reason other than price why they would not sign there and then?

A good question - not cheeky - but he left knowing that he either had to get the price right or overcome a roadblock, be it operational, technical or political. Importantly, he was in control.

When somebody asks you for the price you have choices. Either give them the price quickly and confidently, then stay quiet, or, if it is complex, advise them you will get them a price within say 24 hours. Whatever you do, do not think aloud in front of them; any rambling or waffling will not help your cause!

Final tip - you can possibly solve two challenges with one tactic. The first challenge is winning your first clients; the second is obtaining positive references from them. I have seen a number of people use an "early adopter" strategy to good effect, e.g. "If I offer you an early adopter price, discounted from my full rate, would you be prepared, assuming you are satisfied with my product or service, to act as a reference site and allow me to put a testimonial on my website"?

Delivery

We really covered this under "Characteristics of a Successful Business" in the Reflection Phase.

The key, if you recall, is to follow a process which enables you to have satisfied clients, who either buy from you again or refer other people to you.

Just remember, every time you are in contact with a client, your aim should be to ensure that it is a positive experience.

VBS Business Plan
KPIs

- *Monthly billable days growing from 4 (Q1) to 8(Q2) to 12 (Q3) to 16 (Q4)*

- *Revenue run rate correspondingly increasing from £3k (Q1) to £6k (Q2) to £9k (Q3) to £12k (Q4) – total £30k*

- *Costs contained to 20% of turnover - £6k*

- *Pipeline value at end of each quarter > next quarter forecast*

- *Liquidity ratio of 1.5:1*

Figure 3.8

Monitoring

We now need to keep the business on track! On the facing page we have some Key Performance Indicators or KPIs. (Figure 3.8). To use a medical drama analogy, what happens in a medical soap is that a nurse comes around to the patient's bed, checks temperature, pulse, blood pressure etc, scribbles something on a chart, adds the time and her initials, and moves on. If she is worried she takes immediate action and calls for reinforcements. You need the same for your business; you need to know if your business has lapsed into a coma without you noticing. KPIs will help you to do that.

So we can now do the KPIs for your business. These tally with the numbers in the Profit and Loss Forecast and Cash Flow Forecast we created earlier (Figures 2.13 and 2.14). We have five KPIs; billable days, corresponding revenue run rates, cost control, pipeline value, and liquidity ratio (this is what we have in the bank, plus what we are owed, against what we owe).

The next chart (Figure 3.9) is a "Flash Report" for your sixth month of trading, again based on the Profit and Loss Forecast and Cash Flow Forecast we created earlier; this, together with the KPIs, helps us to check that we are on track. Let's imagine for a moment we do a check at six

VBS Limited
Monthly Financial Reporting

Month 6

	Flash Report	Budget
Financial results		
Sales	£2,400	£2,000
Cost of Sales	£0	£0
Gross Profit	£2,400	£2,000
Overhead	£400	£400
Net Profit	£2,000	£1,600
Reserve	£500	£400
Dividend	£1,500	£1,200
KPIs		
Billable DayRate	£200	£250
Revenue Run Rate	12 days	8 days
Costs	£400	£400
Pipeline	£12,000	>£9,000
Liquidity Ratio	10:1	1.5:1

Figure 3.9

months with some illustrative numbers. If you remember we wanted to be on a run rate by this stage of eight billable days a month at £250 per day. The bad news is we are only getting £200 per day but we are doing 12 days. So we are ahead of our first two KPIs. Further good news - we have kept our costs to less than 20% of turnover; our pipeline is fractionally ahead of the next quarter, which also good news.

And finally our liquidity ratio is very healthy. Remember what this means is that you look at what you have in the bank, add to that what you are owed, take off what you owe and hope that the ratio is better than 1:1 i.e. if the business stopped on that day you would be in a good position to pay all your liabilities as they fell due. If it was the other way round, you would only be surviving with the goodwill of the bank and your creditors. We have checked, and you are not in a coma, so we can press ahead. If the KPIs and the Flash Report had shown something worrying, we could have taken immediate action.

VBS Business Plan
Action Plan

- *Incorporate, open bank account, create website and network database, sort legal documentation (pre-launch)*

- *Set up all processes, plus KPI monitoring (Q1)*

- *Implement quality control checks (Q2)*

- *Assemble product/service toolkit (Q3)*

- *Review progress and create Year 2 plan (Q4)*

Figure 3.10

As a lead in to actually launching your business, we can now complete the Action Plan part of your one-pager. You will see this on the facing page (Figure 3.10). I have highlighted five key action points - it will be better to attempt to do five things really well than 20 averagely! A few comments on each of the five parts;

- These are all things you need to have done before you launch, to help you embark on your journey with confidence.
- You need to be working to a sales and delivery process from the start of your first operating month. The KPI monitoring (see later) can follow at the end of the month.
- Towards the end of the second quarter you need to take soundings from your early clients that they are happy with your product or service.
- By the third quarter you will have a better feel for the range of services/products you can offer, based on early client feedback.
- In the final quarter you need to take stock and create your plan for year 2!

VBS One-Page Plan
Figure 3.11

Strategy	Marketing and Sales	Operations	Finance
- Vision – "Achieving Growth through Trust"	- Simple but compelling pitch	- Business structure based on "cornerstones" principles	- 16 billable days per month (by year-end)
- Core business - providing virtual support to the SME market	- Dynamic website with supporting collateral	- Robust contractual documentation	- Rate average of £250 per day
- Business objective – to be the trusted provider of choice……	- Sales Qualification Process	- Simple but effective CRM system	- No dilution by external associates so 100% gross profit
- Business strategy - …by building trusted relationships and exceeding client expectations	- Pipeline Process	- Delivery Process to maximise repeat business and quality referrals	- Total costs to be contained at 20% of turnover
- Key Success Factor – maximising networks	- Conversion Ratio Process	- Culture of quality control (client reviews and business improvement reviews)	- Lifestyle business

KPI's

- Monthly billable days growing from 4 (Q1) to 8 (Q2) to 12 (Q3) to 16 (Q4)
- Revenue run rate correspondingly increasing from £3k (Q1) to £6k (Q2) to £9k (Q3) to £12k (Q4) – total £30k
- Costs contained to 20% of turnover - £6k
- Pipeline value at end of each quarter > next quarter forecast
- Liquidity ratio of 1.5:1

Action Plan

- Incorporate, open bank account , create website, and network database, sort legal documentation (Pre-launch)
- Set up all processes, plus KPI monitoring (Q1)
- Implement quality control checks (Q2)
- Assemble product/service toolkit (Q3)
- Review progress and create Year 2 plan (Q4)

We can now see what the one page plan looks like when all the components are assembled (Figure 3.11).

You now have your operational map and route for year 1.

SELF-DIAGNOSTIC THREE
Are you finished with your launch phase?

NO	ISSUE	SCORE out of 10
1	Have you chosen your preferred vehicle and sorted your bank account?	
2	Have you reviewed your infrastructure requirements?	
3	Have you worked out your pricing policy?	
4	Are you clear how many routes to market you have?	
5	Have you a networking plan?	
6	Have you established your marketing mix?	
7	Have you explored early adopter possibilities?	
8	Have you created an operating plan for year 1?	
9	Have you established your Key Performance Indicators?	
10	Are you happy you can fund the business through year 1?	
TOTAL		

Score < 30   *You may want to delay launch*

Score < 60   *You may want to opt for a soft launch while you complete your hard launch plans*

Score > 60   *You probably have enough momentum to proceed with a hard launch.*

SELF DIAGNOSTIC THREE

You are now ready to take the third test (facing page) – are you ready to hard launch?

Value Chain Model

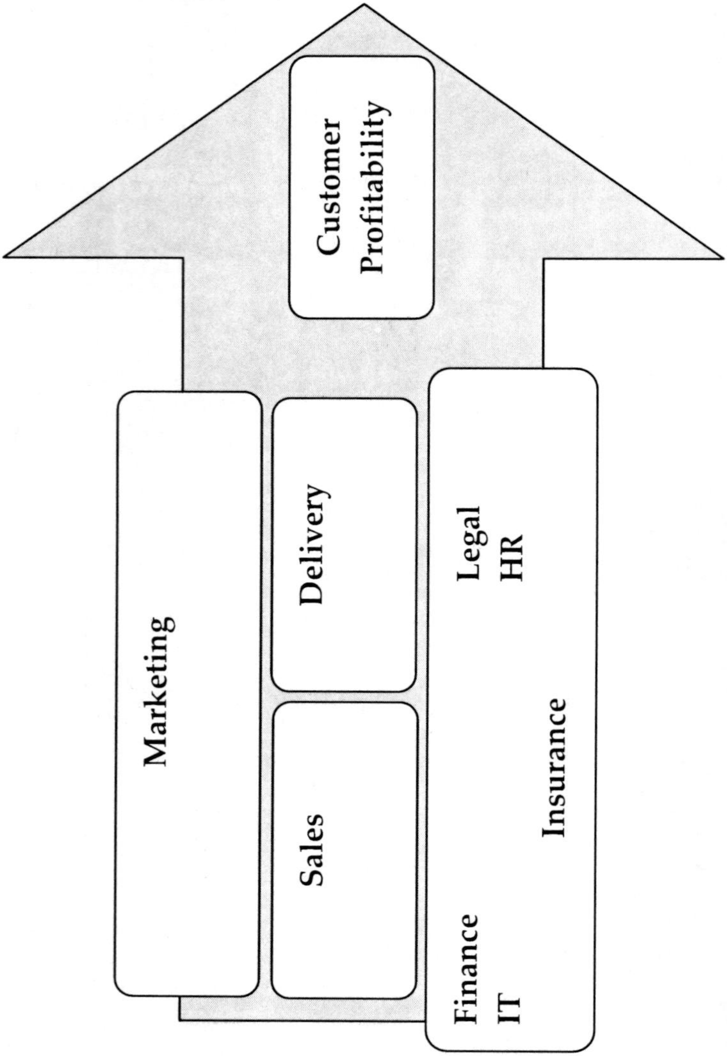

Customer Profitability

Marketing

Delivery

Sales

Legal
HR

Insurance

Finance
IT

Figure 4.1

Epilogue ...

I hope you have found the book helpful. I want to leave you with a final diagram (Figure 4.1) to help you remember the salient points:

- Marketing is not a one-off exercise - it goes on forever. Make sure people understand what makes you different, and make sure you live up to it. If your market moves, make sure you move with it.
- It's all about clients (Sales) and satisfying them (Delivery) so that they come back for more and/or recommend others.
- Don't forget to invest in the Infrastructure (Finance, Legal, IT, HR, Insurance) to make your business a well-oiled machine.
- And finally, do not lose sight of what makes you and your business special; that should be represented in the profitability to you of your customers and therefore your profit margin!

Now, in the words of an old western movie;

"Go get 'em"
Good Luck!

APPENDIX
Top Tips

Tops Tips for start ups - Legal

The Legal Director
Directing legal affairs for businesses

1. Dealing with Lawyers

It is likely you will need to use a lawyer at some point in your start up phase. Make sure you understand what you are asking your lawyer to do, and what you will and won't pay for, and push for a fixed fee. Don't be afraid to say if you think you're not getting value for money. The best business lawyers can be a real asset to your growing business and become a trusted advisor. Ask for a package deal that includes support on ad hoc queries over the first few months of trading (note that you may be able to access this kind of legal support service through membership of organisations like the IoD or your local Chamber of Commerce).

2. Business name

Is anyone else already trading with a similar name? Check the business name you want to use is available as a website domain and (if you are going to incorporate a company or LLP) at Companies House. Even if the exact one you want is available avoid names that could be confused with an existing business.

197

3. Data Protection

Register your new business with the Information Commissioner's Office www.ico.gov.uk and make sure you understand the rules on handling personal data.

4. Business Plan

Does your business plan contain confidential or proprietary information about your products or services? Include an appropriate disclaimer and confidentiality statement on the first page, and in the footer "© [Name] Ltd, 2010. Confidential." Consider whether you should ask recipients to sign a specific confidentiality agreement.

5. Founders' Agreement

If your business has more than one founder, then whether you are a company, LLP or partnership you ought to have a properly drafted shareholders/partnership agreement. If not you will be bound by the default regime in the relevant legislation which may not be appropriate for your situation. Think of it as a "pre-nup": what to expect from your partners, how are you going to run the business on a day to day basis, and what will you do if you fall out?

6.   Terms and Conditions

You will need properly prepared terms and conditions for dealing with your customers/clients. Make sure you understand what your obligations are in terms of the quality of your products or standard of service, delivery, and refunds.

Always insist on trading with your customers on your own terms and conditions.

7.   Distance Selling

If you are selling to consumers (B2C) over the internet or phone you will need to comply with distance selling regulations that specify what information you must give to customers, and an unconditional right to cancel and get a full refund in the first seven days. See www.berr.gov.uk/whatwedo/consumers/buying-selling/distance-selling/index.html

8.   Consumer Credit Licenses

If you are dealing with consumers (B2C) and either hiring goods for more than 3 months, or selling on hire purchase, or offering other credit terms you may need a Consumer Credit License. See   www.oft.gov.uk/advice_and_resources/resource_base/credit-licence/requiring

9. Raising Money

If you are looking to raise money from investors you need to make sure you don't fall foul of the rules on financial promotions - what you can say and to whom. If you get it wrong your investors can ask for their money back so this is one area where you should obtain specialist advice.

10. Intellectual Property

Keep your know-how and proprietary data safe and use a confidentiality agreement if you are going to disclose it. Is it important that you stop others copying your ideas, products or services? Applying for patents and trademarks is expensive and can take a long time and only effective if you are prepared to enforce (very expensive and time-consuming). You can use the ™ symbol without registering a trademark, although it has no legal significance in the UK.

Tops Tips for start ups - Accounting

1.   Tax Structure

Sole Trader vs. Limited Company vs. Partnership. If you are starting a business, it is important to ensure that you choose the right tax structure. There are advantages and disadvantages to each of the different tax structures, and it is therefore important that you obtain advice from an accountant as to the most suitable structure for your current circumstances, business plan and future goals.

2.   Registering for VAT

If you're a business and the goods or services you provide count as what's known as 'taxable supplies' you'll have to register for VAT if either your turnover for the previous 12 months has gone over a specific limit - called the 'VAT threshold' (currently £68,000) or if you think your turnover will soon reach this limit, however you can voluntarily register for VAT if you would like to. There are different VAT schemes, annual VAT (which means you only need to submit a VAT return once a year), normal VAT on an accrual basis (returns are submitted quarterly, based on invoice date), normal VAT on a cash basis (returns will be submitted quarterly, based on when you have received/ paid the money), the Flat Rate VAT scheme (a set percentage of your gross turnover is payable). It is important to ensure you register for the best VAT scheme suitable to your circumstances, so ensure to obtain advice regarding this from your accountant.

3. Filing Responsibilities of a Limited Company

If you are a limited company, you will be responsible for submitting a set of abbreviated financial accounts to Companies House nine months after your accounting period end date and a full set of financial accounts together with your corporation tax return to HMRC 12 months after your accounting period end date. You are also required to complete an annual return to Companies House (annual shuttle return) each year; this can be completed online or via a paper return, and is normally due 12 months after incorporation. You can register your business on Business Link's website and they will remind you of your filing obligations via email (https://www.businesslink.gov.uk/bdotg/ action/keyDatesAlert).

4. Personal Tax Returns & Deadlines

If you are self-employed, a director of a limited company, if you have rental income, or if you owe HMRC tax on any other source of income, then you are required to complete a personal tax return for the financial year (6th April – 5th April). Your tax return will be due for submission by the 31st October if you are filing a paper return, or by the 31st January of the following year if you are submitting it online. Your tax payment for the year will be payable by the 31st January, together with a 50% payment on account towards your next year's tax liability with the other 50% payable on the 31st July of the following year.

5. Claimable Expenses

All expenses incurred wholly, exclusively and necessarily for business purposes can be claimed through the company or deducted from your sole trader income. Please ensure to keep all receipts/invoices for any expenses incurred. Please note that certain expenses can be paid through the business, however are not tax deductible, i.e. Entertainment, and will therefore be added back when calculating Corporation Tax.

6.   Employing Staff

If you are considering employing staff, you will be required to set-up and administer a PAYE scheme with HMRC - which you can outsource. You will have to calculate PAYE/NI on all payments that an employee receives, and you will need to make these payments to HMRC by the 19th of the following month. You will also be required to provide all employees employed at the 5th of April with a P60 by the 31st May following the end of the tax year or a P45 when an employee leaves your employment. You will also be responsible to file a P35 & P14 (payroll year end returns) to HMRC by 19th May each year, form P11d (Benefits & Expenses) to HMRC by the 6th July each year.

7.   Credit Control

In any successful business CASH IS KING, and therefore it is imperative that credit control is exercised frequently. Work together with your accounting function (in-house or outsourced) to set these controls and procedures in place and prepare a monthly cash flow statement to ensure you will be able to meet your short-term and long-term liabilities.

8.   Paperwork & Filing

You are required to keep a paper trail of all invoices, expenses, bank statements, credit cards etc. for a minimum of six years. Ensure that your filing is kept up to date and we recommend filing all invoices in sequential order and all supplier invoices per supplier which will make it easier to obtain paperwork in future. It is also advisable to write on the paperwork to which account it has been posted and the date is was entered and paid.

9.   Accounting Packages

It is advisable to enter your accounting records and transactions into an accounting package from day one, as it will assist you in obtaining useful management information efficiently and effectively and it will reduce your accountant's fee for preparing your statutory accounts at year end. QuickBooks and SAGE are widely used amongst small to medium-sized companies; however it is advised to obtain advice from an accountant as to the most beneficial accounting package to suit your particular circumstances, type of business and your long-term goals.

10. Accounting Function

In-house or Outsourced. There are advantages and disadvantages to both, however outsourcing the accounting function for small to medium sized businesses can be very beneficial, providing the following benefits amongst others: expert services at a fraction of the price, no recruitment/ management fees, no office expenses, continuity is provided with no need for re-hiring or re-training and many more. It is important to review both options and choose the most optimum solution for your business.

peoplerisksolutions

1. Recruitment

You are bound to need people working with you in your new business. Recruiting the right individuals is important. A good place to start is using your network to identify known candidates. You could also place adverts online - there are several cost effective job boards which can harvest lots of CVs. Bear in mind that if you get someone with 75% of the skills you need you are doing well. If you still don't find someone then use a recruitment agency, but make sure that you negotiate a good fee rate upfront. Always carry out thorough interviews and ensure that you draw up a list of competencies and skills that you want for the job.

2. Reference checks

Once you have identified the right person make sure you carry out independent reference checks before they join. Many people are not completely honest on their CVs. Do not accept previously written "To whom it may concern" references. Always contact previous employers. You may wish to conduct a criminal records bureau (CRB) check as well - this website may be helpful www.crb.gov.uk. There are also agencies who offer a full reference service such as www.kroll.com.

3. Pay

An important part of the business dynamic is how much to pay yourself and your team. Take advice from your accountants regarding tax because this will drive the pay structure. Make sure that you appoint someone competent to run your payroll and to manage issues like PAYE, P60s and P45s. Pay is likely to be one of your largest overheads and so make sure that you do not overpay staff. Try and be creative such as offering commission for increased sales so that your increased income can improve pay for some staff.

4. Employment contracts

If you employ staff make sure that you give them some form of employment contract. This should lay out key aspects of employment such as salary, notice period, holidays, benefits, disciplinary and grievance procedures. There are several HR outsource businesses that can provide low cost help such as HR Advantage – www.hradvantage.co.uk. The main aim of the contract is to avoid any misunderstandings later on.

5. Organisational Structure

Most small firms have a fairly flat reporting structure. However, as you employ more people it is important to be clear about who does what and who is responsible for what. A brief job description for each job including who the individual reports into will avoid problems later on. This will also help when you appraise performance.

6. Policies and procedures

It will be useful to have some basic people policies and procedures once you employ more than two or three staff. The main reason is to try and capture all the small employment issues before they arise. A staff handbook can outline how you will deal with issues such as maternity leave, disciplinary issues, compassionate leave, benefits and any restrictions post employment. As the business grows you can add policies as appropriate.

7. Performance management

Most people want to know how they are performing at work. You should have some form of performance appraisal process. As a minimum formally appraise everyone at least once a year. Use company and individual objectives to ensure that everyone's efforts are focussed in the same direction. Also take into account learning and development for your team. Improving skills will end up adding value to the business overall.

8.   Dealing with disputes

When you employ people there will inevitably be disputes. Make sure that you always treat everyone fairly and be consistent when dealing with problems. Make sure that you follow due process if you have to discipline anyone - failure to do so can be regarded as unfair and claims can be made accordingly via an employment tribunal. The ACAS website is helpful in this regard - www.acas.org.uk

9.   Non-executive Directors

As the business grows it is worthwhile appointing non-executive directors. These are typically people who have expertise and can advise you on how to take the business forward. Initially they may be unpaid but in due course you should pay them a nominal fee.

10. Succession planning

In order to ensure business growth you should plan for changes of personnel. People leave firms for a range of unexpected reasons so it is worth thinking about who could replace key roles. Some entrepreneurs are always interviewing potential candidates in order to keep the people pipeline alive. It is also important to provide development opportunities where possible.

Tops Tips for start ups - Information Technology

Network Maintenance Limited

1.   IT Budget

Budgeting and choosing the right equipment for the tasks that are required at the beginning, and that will be useful in the future for your Business, is fundamental. Many small businesses do not realise the competitive advantages offered by technology, as they don't have the resources or expertise to evaluate or implement the solutions available to them. Another key problem is that many people try to spend as little as possible on technology and therefore disregard the potential cost savings that can be generated if they get it right.

Investment into IT systems is important and below are some key points relating to investment.

2.   Creating an Internet Identity

Domain name and email addresses should be the first thing you think about, choose an unused domain name and register it with a professional organisation who can offer multiple email accounts and web/storage space. Choose a domain name relevant to the name of the company or a name which directly relates to the company's type of business; this will help later to self promote your website on search engines.

From the chosen office location organise an internet connection; research the suppliers available to you at that location – e.g. BT, O2 or Virgin; there are deals and discounts available when you combine internet and telephone services through the same supplier.

3.   Protecting your identity

If your business uses email, you'll be targeted at some stage. The main problem is that such attacks are becoming more sophisticated. The malicious software used develops in your system and the threat of someone accessing valuable company information becomes more likely.

Fraudulent emails are increasingly authentic in appearance, purporting to originate from various sources, from banks to potential clients. The process is known as "Phishing", and such emails will contain a link to a website on which you will be asked to re-confirm some details or confirm a password, with the aim of stealing your details and using them to access your account. Files coming into an organisation downloaded from the internet and transported on a flash drive or disc for example, can also be dangerous. These can contain malicious software, generally known as malware, that is sophisticated enough to hide itself from anti-virus software. Malware can log any key strokes that you make on the keyboard and send the information elsewhere when you connect to the web. This means that passwords and bank account details could be at risk, along with private company documents and emails.

It is recommended that you have a company policy to deal with such issues. Education and awareness for staff about the dangers out there is all important and for most organisations it is the first line of defence. It is as much the responsibility of the individual employee as it is for management to be aware of identity fraud and protect their own and the company's interests. This could mean regulating the use of external hard drives, including iPods, flash keys and discs with dubious or uncertain origins in the workplace and, moreover, informing staff of the ways in which criminals might try to access their private information.

Data leakage is also an increasing problem. For businesses, corporate identity is as precious as their staff and preventing information from getting out could be down to something as simple as warning people not to share too much on social networking websites or not to send too much valuable company information across the internet.

4.   Router and Firewall

Purchase a good brand wireless router - this may come free with the internet connection. Ensure that it has a built in firewall, as this will help to secure any equipment that will be connected to the internet. The router creates the connection automatically between your network and the internet via your ISP - Internet Service Provider. A router, rather than just a modem, is used because it uses NAT – Network Address Translation as part of its Firewall. This works by converting (translating) the internet address, TCPIP protocol, to a private address range on the inside of your network.

Anyone trying to attack the external address will not be able to penetrate the firewall unless there are ports open to let traffic through.

5.   Network

For a small network, the router that the ISP supplies will probably suffice, as it will usually come with four Ethernet Ports (normally 100MB).

In addition the router will normally be wireless enabled, which can be connected to a plethora of different devices – PC's, Laptops, wireless printers, PDA's, Phones and Games consoles.

If you require more than four hard wired devices then a small Gigabit network switch would be ideal, with 5 to 48 ports on a single switch, desk to switches 5 to 16 ports and rack mountable switches available from 16 to 48 ports. These switches are available in many price ranges and complex abilities, for larger organisations they may use PoE – Power over Ethernet switches which can power IP telephones, wireless access points, cameras and many other PoE enabled devices.

6.   Server

For small and large networks it is important to have a server to centrally store the company's data. For fast response and resilient availability, choose and design your server to cope with the company's immediate needs. In the future storage can always be added on should it be required.

If the server is to run databases such as SQL or similar, make sure that the processor is well above the stated minimum specification for the application. Memory for servers is more expensive than for standard PC's but it is very important to have enough for the server to comfortably run all of the systems it has to. If a server runs light on memory, it will slow down and use the hard disks to swap information that it is required and this will make the server slow to respond and will shorten the life of the hard drives.

7. Software

When installing Software onto a computer system you can never be too careful, especially if you keep important customer information stored there. Even if the software has come from a trusted source, complications can arise and it would be wise to take precautions beforehand. It's always best, therefore, to make a back-up copy of important information before installing any new software.

You should try to scan all floppy disks, CD-ROMs, and DVD-ROMs with your anti-virus software before copying files from them or installing software that they contain. You never know if a nasty virus is lurking on a seemingly innocent disk.

Never install pirated software onto your computer. Illegal copies of software, such as those downloaded from hacker websites or sourced from file-sharing programs, may contain hidden viruses.

Before installing any software, be sure you know exactly what is being copied onto your system. Sometimes apparently innocuous software can contain viruses or 'Trojans' that might take control of your computer. This is a particular danger with file-sharing programs that allow you to trade music or videos.

8. Antivirus

Antivirus protection also plays an important role as it should safeguard you from the harmful Viruses, Spyware and those annoying spammed messages on your email. There are many free and paid for antivirus products available on the market but it is important to make sure that the one you chose is adequate for your needs and that you have it running up-to-date on all of you computers.

You should regularly check and scan your computers for Viruses and Spyware, as many infections are designed to steal your identity and passwords and can appear like Trojans at any time.

In addition, you should be careful when registering to anything online that it is provided by reputable company and that you are on a secure website. This is always indicated by the address starting with https:// or a locked padlock somewhere on your browser application. It is sometimes a good idea to use a temporary or online mail account when subscribing to an unknown source, so that your normal mail data is protected should the new source turn out to be bogus.

9.   UPS

Protecting your hardware from power spikes and disturbances is important. Laptops are usually alright as they predominately run on their own internal battery. PCs, servers, routers and other network components will require mains filtering and battery backup, as data corruption or loss can occur if the power is lost or spiked to your equipment. UPS (Uninterruptable Power Suppliers) are available in all sizes and affordability but don't scrimp on these. Ideally you would want it to stay running for at least 10 minutes, in order to give you a chance to save that important document that you have spent hours working on. Basic multiport units are available, which can maintain power for a few devices that would possibly loose data if the power was to fail. Recommended devices to be protected would be PCs and servers; other devices such as printers network switches and routers do not require UPS protection but will require surge protection to protect them from spikes and mains interference.

10.   Backup

A small network should have at least one form of data backup e.g. Tape, CD/DVD, External Hard Disk or Offsite Backup. It is not ideal to keep all your data in one place where it can be vulnerable to fire, theft or data corruption. It is always recommended that you keep a copy of your data in a physically different location to the work place, so that should the original data be lost, it can be replaced easily.

There are now many organisations and ISP's who can supply you with off-site or internet based backups and most of these work very well, utilising your internet bandwidth at night when your requirement to use this is less. Always make sure that with whatever backup you choose that you regularly check the logs and periodically perform data restores from whatever source you have chosen, in order to verify that the backup is working and so that you understand how to do this in the event of actually needing the data back.

There are ten common mistakes made with technology in the work place:

1. Assuming that IT can be easily deployed and managed without expert support
2. Failing to test equipment thoroughly with real life scenarios
3. Poor testing of security vulnerabilities
4. Not setting out service requirements with IT providers at the outset
5. Ineffectively aligning IT to business needs
6. Focusing on short term cost gains due to

time pressures and not the longer term productivity and revenue generating benefits of IT

7. Choosing IT that cannot cope with rapid changes in business needs

8. Not planning ahead so you can scale up your technology needs appropriately

9. Having the wrong return on investment expectations of technology which impacts badly on the bottom line

10. Cutting IT budget or thinking managing IT in-house will be easier and more cost effective in hard times

Choosing the right hardware and software is Key to success when integrating IT into your new business.

Tops Tips for start ups - Insurance

KNIGHTHOOD
Corporate Assurance Services plc

Insurance is a vital part of any business trading armoury.

Below are a number of handy tips you should consider when assessing what insurance is most appropriate for you and your business but probably the most important part is to understand the whole basis of insurance. It is, in simple terms, "risk transfer". You are asking somebody else to bear the burden of some of the risks – mainly financial – that you would be unable to assume in your own right. For example, few businesses would be able to reconstruct, say, their building or replace all of their stock if either were to be destroyed in a fire.

Also, few businesses would be able to withstand the financial strain of dealing with a liability claim against them where, dependent upon damages involved, the claim could run into hundreds of thousands if not millions of pounds.

To arrange for a third party to accept the risk on your behalf you must pay them an annual fee. The third party is known as the insurer or underwriter and the fee is known as the insurance premium.

More importantly, the third party will expect you to take all reasonable steps to minimise the possibility of a loss and positive Risk Management is usually rewarded with lower premiums.

Insurance protects the financial investment you have made in your business and is therefore often described as providing "peace of mind". Unfortunately, it is not possible to insure the other investment in your business such as time, family sacrifices, energy and emotion!

To help you get through the maze of insurance, here are some handy tips:

1. Carefully select a broker

Ask friends or family or industry peers if they are able to recommend a Broker. Perhaps see two or three different firms for advice and quotations and compare who is most responsive to your needs. Ensure that they come and see you and inspect your premises or at least meet with you so that they may help identify some of the risks you face in your business.

Ask them exactly what services they provide and try to agree some service standard levels that meet your demands. Ensure they fully understand your business and ask them who will be looking after you in an ongoing capacity if you were to appoint them.

Ask them if they would help you in the event of claims, and if so how would they do it.

It is possible to buy online but there can be pitfalls. Informed, face to face advice is very often the better option.

2.   Make sure you get written quotations

Make sure you are supplied with full details of all Terms and Conditions that will apply, before giving instructions to go on cover. Read all documents carefully and ensure that you are able to comply in full. If you cannot you should let your broker know.

3.   Work with the Broker to carefully assess your own risk

There is no benefit to over insuring and to under insure could leave you in serious financial difficulties, so make sure all of your sums insured are carefully calculated.

Similarly, make sure you have accurate estimates of your turnover and projected wages and estimated gross profits, etc.

4.   Professional Risks

In addition to obvious business exposures such as asset protection, etc, it is important that you consider professional risks which could, amongst other things, include financial covers such as Directors & Offices insurance, Libel and Slander insurance, Fidelity insurance, Trustees Indemnity and the like.

5.   Make sure you meet your legal requirements

You are required by law to have Employers Liability insurance. This is required by Statute and you will face penalties if you do not have the correct insurance.

Similarly if you operate cars, vans, lorries or other motorised equipment on a public highway you are required to arrange Third Party insurance under the requirements of the Road Traffic Act.

6.   Make sure you are aware of contractual requirements

In addition to insurances which you must arrange by statute, you may also find yourself asked to have in place, or effect, certain covers as part of a contractual arrangement. These normally relate to Professional Indemnity which, in short, offers cover for financial loss arising out of errors or omissions in your advice.

Such contracts can also ask for Public Liability insurance and, if appropriate, Products Liability insurance.

It is worth noting that these covers are often basic requirements of contracts with local authorities and other public bodies.

7. Consider your Own Risk Profile and Manage Your Risk

Insurers will often allow discounts if you are agreeable to a deductible to be applied to your policy. You may also select to self-insure in some instances and you should discuss the options available to you in depth with your selected broker in establishing your own risk profile.

Insurers will normally reward a well run business with lower premiums as good housekeeping and good risk management will minimise their potential exposure to claims. Always try to follow your industry's best practice standards and also ensure you comply with the requirements of Health and Safety legislation and guidance. Always do your best to discharge your duty of care to all Third Parties as well as your moral obligation for the safety and wellbeing of your staff.

8.   Budget Your Costs Correctly

Remember that expenditure in respect of insurance may not be limited to the cost of the premium being asked to enable the risk transfer. You should also budget to include the following, as relevant to your particular trade:-

- Fire extinguishing appliances
- Good quality door locks and window locks
- Other physical security such as bars or grills
- Health & Safety consultancy and implementation
- An intruder alarm
- CCTV
- Staff training
- A fire alarm

9.   Review Your Arrangements Regularly

When you have worked with your Broker to design an insurance programme that matches your needs and budget do not consider that an end to the matter.

All businesses alter over a period of time maybe by changing their business focus or acquiring extra staff or vehicles. Newer businesses tend to change more frequently and you should therefore make sure your Broker is aware of all developments so that he may advise you accordingly.

10. Further Financial Advice

Make sure your Insurance Broker is able to offer other financial advice which would protect your business or find an Independent Financial Adviser who is skilled in the needs of a business. They should be able to advise you on, for example, insuring important people in your business (Key Man Assurance) and protecting the shareholdings of investors in your business (Share Purchase Assurance). They should also be able to help you out with such things as Employee Benefits, typically Group Life Insurance, Group Private Medical Insurance, Health Insurance and the like.

Gordon Westcott is the Development Manager of Knighthood Corporate Assurance Services plc (Company Registration Number 1194084).

Knighthood is authorised and regulated by the Financial Services Authority (FSA), Authorisation Reference 126707.

Other Useful Reading

Ashton R (2004) *The Entrepreneur's Book of Checklists* (Pearson)

Carter M. (2004) *It's All Cobblers* (Management Books)

Essential Business (2008) *The Essential Business Guide* (3rd edition) (Ashford Press)

Gerber M. (2001) *The E-Myth Revisited* (HarperCollins)

Lambert T. (2001) *High Income Consulting* (Nicholas Brealey)

Southon M. And West C. (2005) *Sales on a Beermat* (Random House)

Southon M. And West C. (2004) *The Beermat Entrepreneur* (Random House)

Warnes B (1994) *The Genghis Khan Guide to Business* (12th edition) (Osmosis)

Weiss A (2000) *Getting started in Consulting* (Wiley)

Williams S. (2003) *Small Business Guide* (16th edition) (Press Vitesse)